ENDORSEMENTS

"Coach Brian White is what makes college football great. Generations of players have found the very best in coaching from him—a true servant leader that drives others to achieve their fullest potential. Coach White excited passion, love, and respect for both his players and the game they play. Though he entered my life through the game of football, his teachings and impact have far surpassed the bounds of the game."

- ANDY STRADER, *former BC football player & 2019 Scanlan Award winner*

"Coach White's book captures exactly what makes the game special. It's about people, trust, and the bonds that last a lifetime! The locker room really isn't for sale, and nobody tells that story better than him."

- AJ DILLON, *Philadelphia Eagles RB and former Boston College All Time Leading Rusher*

"I first met Coach Brian White at my alma mater, Bowling Green, and it didn't take long to see his impact on everyone around him. His deep knowledge of the game is matched only by his ability to connect with people on a personal level. What I admire most is how he uses his emotional intelligence to guide and inspire, shaping athletes and men who become leaders in their communities and lives. Coach White's legacy extends far beyond football—it's written in the character of those he has influenced. *The Locker Room is Not For Sale* should be mandatory reading for any leader in any walk of life!"

- JOHN KAPLAN, *Co-Founder, Force Management*

Brian White translates decades of sideline wisdom into advice for every leader. Protect the locker room, celebrate the right things, and make hard calls with compassion will make every culture and team better. If you are a leader read this book, connect with your team and win together!

— **JON GORDON,** *18x best-selling author of* The Energy Bus *and* The 7 Commitments of a Great Team.

THE LOCKER ROOM IS NOT FOR SALE

THE LOCKER ROOM IS NOT FOR SALE

WHY THE HUMAN TOUCH ALWAYS WINS

BRIAN WHITE

THE LOCKER ROOM IS NOT FOR SALE
Why the Human Touch Always Wins

Copyright © 2026 by Brian White

Cover Design by Alex Kirkland
Interior Layout and Design by Brittany Becker
Editorial Team: Jeffrey Miller, Ginny Glass, Jamie Smith, Rachel Maier

ISBNs:
Ebook: 979-8-89165-367-2
Paperback: 979-8-89165-368-9
Hardcover: 979-8-89165-369-6

Published by:
Gordon Publishing
Kansas City, MO
gordonpublishing.com

To my wife, Salli, who really puts the exclamation point on "the human touch always wins"! Thank you for allowing me to live in my world of "perpetual recess" while you poured your soul into raising our two wonderful children, Cassi and Jackson. You sacrificed an amazing career filled with celebrities for the joy of leading our family. I can only hope you know how much I admire and love you. Thank you. Recess has been a blast!

CONTENTS

FOREWORD

WHEN MY GREAT friend Brian White told me he had written a book and wanted me to write the foreword, I realized that the only way to do so was to go back to the beginning.

So here we go. I met Brian (henceforth Whitey) freshman week at Harvard in 1982. I can still remember the first time I saw him. He had a "wiffle" (a Boston term for a crewcut) and was walking through Harvard Yard wearing hospital pants, a half shirt, turf shoes, carrying an ice cream cone in one hand and a football in the other. From day one, he had one word written all over him: "Coach."

Over the next few years, despite the fact that we had a suite of rooms for our rooming group of eight people in G10 of Leverett Towers, Whitey and I always somehow got stuck in the same room together. We used to talk all the time about what we wanted to do, where we wanted to go, and more precisely, how we wanted to be great—at something. That was always the goal. To be great. And even though we were surrounded by wealth and privilege, money was never the measure of greatness or the motivation for either of us. Maybe because we never had any, and if we did, it went to cheesesteaks, tickets to films, or the latest Nike gear.

What it came down to was that we both wanted to do something different. The goal was to try to use whatever talents you had to inspire other people to chase their own dreams. After many years and much questioning, I got into film, but for Whitey there was never any doubt. More than anyone I've ever met, Whitey knew exactly what he wanted to do. He was going to be a coach. It ran so deep in his blood that the temptations a Harvard quarterback is offered from Wall Street upon graduation bounced off of him like so many errant passes.

I clearly remember one night sitting around with a group of former teammates, and everyone was talking about the world of finance. I looked over at Whitey, and he looked like a lightbulb someone had just unscrewed. Then, for some reason, someone started talking about football, and Whitey lit up like a Christmas tree. At that moment, you could see that he almost didn't have a choice. He had made the choice years earlier when, as a young kid, he followed his father, the legendary and late, great Donnie White, onto the fields and into the locker rooms of all the teams that Donnie had coached.

Although I knew Donnie had been the quarterback at Notre Dame years earlier, I didn't realize exactly how deep the football and coaching genes ran in Whitey's family until his wedding to the incredible Salli in Las Vegas in the mid-'90s. At the rehearsal dinner, Donnie White stood up, grabbed the microphone, and proudly announced, "We are a football family." All of the Whites were at the head table with him as they launched into every fight song of every team they had ever played for or coached. I think they finished the last remaining fight song the next day, a couple of hours before the wedding.

As I read Whitey's book, two words struck me: *passion* and *authenticity*. As someone who makes films, I know nothing great ever happens without passion. It is the raison d'être, and nothing can replace it. It is what moves you when there is every reason not to move. The other word is *authenticity*. This is what moves others to follow you. You cannot fake either one, and you cannot lead without them. Whitey's coaching career is defined by these two words, and the lessons in this book and the integrity of the messenger are uniquely and profoundly personal.

Case in point, I laughed when I read the part about the advice from renowned offensive line Coach Joe Moore, who said to him, "You want to be a great coach? Feed 'em." This rang so true for me because Whitey and food are somehow inseparable. In fact, here's a little-known secret. When we got our first ATM cards at Harvard, the bank teller said to use the first word that came to mind as your password. I imagined Whitey's password would have been "Elway" or something like that, but when I asked him what he chose in light of the teller's suggestion, he leaned over and whispered "food" as if it were a state secret. Food for Whitey, as a coach and person, represents something special. Breaking bread together, like what happens in the locker room, is a sacred rite for him that brings people of every stripe together and knocks down walls.

What I found most fascinating about the book, however, is that it is basically a love letter. A love letter to everyone who influenced him and instilled in him the values that have defined his life. A love letter to all the players he coached who became disciples and shining examples of all that was passed down to him and that he selflessly passed down to them. And a love letter to all the football coaches who first inspired him as a kid and taught him to never give up and always get up when you get knocked down.

But *The Locker Room Is Not For Sale* is about so much more than football. It is a playbook for life, filled with hard-earned wisdom and life lessons, the kind you can only attain through sweat and dirt, victory and defeat, sacrifice and triumph. And what makes this book even more remarkably powerful and poignant is that the man who is sharing these nuggets of gold is battling, and has battled, Parkinson's with grace and courage for the last ten years.

I think at some point in everyone's life, they feel the need to share what they have learned. Otherwise, what is the point? This book is the definition of paying it forward. It celebrates the fact that everyone is a work in progress and a masterpiece waiting to happen, and the job of any great coach or leader is to do just that, lead the way, fearlessly and with undying faith and optimism.

Whitey's father, Donnie, and mother, Maureen, who is also a teacher, passed down generational truths to all their children, and now Whitey has put down his marker. And what a marker it is. It captures all the lessons from a lifetime dedicated to inspiring others and leading the way, and I could not be prouder to be his friend.

Now, I patiently await his next book, *How To Fall Asleep Anywhere at Any Time*, which come to think of it, I may have to cowrite with him.

—FRANK CIOTA

Cofounder, Director, Mavex Films

SACRED SPACE

TO ME, THE locker room represents everything that's right about this country.

It's not just a room with benches and hooks and sweat-soaked jerseys. It's a sanctuary of values, a place where commitment lives. It's where loyalty is tested and brotherhood is forged in the fires of adversity and victory alike. The locker room is team, community, and togetherness. It's the beating heart of everything we hope to be on the field and in life.

I grew up in the locker room. I was raised there by coaches and teammates, and I absorbed the unspoken code that governs those four walls. It taught me how to win, how to lose, how to listen, and when to speak. I learned when to be quiet because the guy next to me was nervous before the biggest game of his life, and I learned when to let loose and celebrate after a hard-fought win. I learned when to put my arm around someone's shoulder and offer nothing but my silent presence after a heartbreaking loss.

In the locker room, I saw so many examples of real leadership. I'm talking about the kind of leaders who lift others up and speak when it counts. You learn quickly who the real ones are, and I'll tell you what, the locker room doesn't suffer phonies for long.

Jerry, the uncle of Jaison Patterson, one of my players last year, told me, "Real is real. Real is rare. And real has no color." That's the locker room. You're either real or you're fake, and the locker room will expose you fast. There's no hiding in there. It's honest, and it's absolutely beautiful. That's why it's a sacred space, and that's why we protect it.

In great locker rooms, there's no faking it. The laughter after a win is real. The tears after a loss are also real. The moments when you look a teammate in the eyes and know he'd go to war for you are real too. It's rare in today's world to find that kind of authenticity anywhere, which is why we guard it so fiercely.

See, the locker room isn't just where we tape our ankles and lace up our cleats. It's where we become family—blood brothers in every way that matters. That kind of bond lasts a lifetime. I'm sixty-one now, nearly four decades removed from my playing days, and the relationships I built in the locker room are still the strongest ones I have.

So when I say the locker room is not for sale, I mean it. You can't buy this. You can't fake it. And if you compromise it by letting ego, politics, or profit invade it, you break something sacred.

This book is my tribute to that space. It's a book for everyone who's ever taped up in silence before a game, for everyone who's ever jumped into a victory pile, for everyone who's ever sat in a circle of worn-down warriors and felt like they belonged to something bigger than themselves. The locker room is where we become who we're meant to be.

In the upcoming chapters, I want to use the values of the locker room as a springboard to give coaches, athletes, and leaders a clear blueprint for lasting success. We'll explore how belief, relentless work, and a rock-solid plan to win turn vision into reality, much like a good coach's pregame speech in the locker room. We'll explore a winning approach to building championship programs, and explore the ways that sports break down barriers, connect people, and create lifelong bonds through the simple, transformative power of human connection.

That's the power of the locker room.

THIRTY-NINE YEARS IN THE GAME AND STILL LEARNING

My thirty-nine-year career started at Fordham University in the Bronx. I was just twenty-two years old when Larry Glueck hired me to coach the running backs. Larry had been an assistant at Harvard when I was playing there, and he took a chance on me when I was fresh out of college. He was a true gentleman, one of the most influential men in my life. Larry used to always tell me, "Never compromise your values." He constantly reminded me, even in a profession that can pull you in every direction, to stay fair and honest, and above all, not to lose who you are in the process.

From Fordham, I made my way to Notre Dame and joined Coach Lou Holtz's staff. We won a national championship there and only lost one game in two years. I was on the sidelines for one of the greatest games in college football history—"Catholics Versus Convicts," the 1988 football game between Notre Dame and Miami. Two rival teams, both undefeated, came together that day in one of the closest games I've ever experienced, and Notre Dame walked away the winner: 31–30.

While the wins were sweet, what I really walked away with was a deeper understanding of what it means to coach. From Coach Holtz, I learned that coaching is the constant conditioning of correct behavior. Coaching is about shaping character, rep after rep, until it becomes second nature—until the lights come on, and your players don't have to think because they just *do*. That's what I call competitive memory, and it's something I still coach to this day.

Then came a move that would change my life in many ways. I flew from Boston to Las Vegas to take an entry-level job at UNLV for $14,000 a year, coaching quarterbacks. I'll never forget sitting on that plane wondering, *What am I doing?* I'd never even seen the desert before. Heck, I didn't know there were mountains in Las Vegas! But that flight was the best decision I ever made. It brought me to my wife, and she gave me my two incredible children. It introduced me to my best friend, Paul "Pooch" Pucciarelli—the legendary equipment manager at UNLV, a locker room guy through and through. You'll hear more about Pooch in these pages because he embodies everything good about this game. After four unforgettable years in Vegas and one in Reno, Barry Alvarez brought me to Wisconsin in 1995. I spent eleven years there and became offensive coordinator in 1999. We built something special at Wisconsin, won two Rose Bowls, and helped shape it into the powerhouse it is today. But what I remember more than the trophies are the people, the locker room moments, and the relationships that lasted long after the game. My kids were born in Madison. My coaching family was built there. Eleven years in one place is rare in this profession, and I don't take it for granted.

After Wisconsin, my career took me to Syracuse as the offensive coordinator. One of the highlights of that stop was coaching alongside my brother, Chris White. For two years, we worked side by side. We didn't win a lot of football games during that stretch, and after my second season, I was given the old "I am going in another direction" line. Time to relocate, but even in the losing, there was something beautiful about sharing that experience with family.

From there, I landed at Washington with Coach Tyrone Willingham. That season, we didn't win a single game. Not one. So let's put that in perspective: I went from a national title at Notre Dame, to Rose Bowls at Wisconsin, to going winless at Washington. That's real life in this profession. It humbles you. Sometimes, it forces you to ask why you're in this to begin with. If you're only coaching for the scoreboard, you won't last long.

Then came an incredible opportunity at the University of Florida. I joined Urban Meyer's staff and later worked under Will Muschamp, spending six seasons coaching and recruiting in the SEC. That conference is as competitive and passionate as it gets. Every week, you're facing the best players in the country. I loved every minute of it. That's a special stage, and it taught me how to sharpen my edge even more and elevate everything: preparation, recruiting, relationships, and locker room culture.

After Florida, I got to come home to Boston College. I spent five years there, working with Steve Addazio, one of my great friends, but the biggest gift of that season of life was being back around my parents. My mom and dad were both teachers and coaches, and my dad was the first coach I ever had. Being near them again after decades of bouncing around the country was a blessing I'll always be grateful for. My foundation was built by them, and being able to share that part of the journey felt like coming full circle.

When our time at BC ended, I headed west to Colorado State. I experienced two years in Fort Collins right in the middle of COVID. It was a strange, uncertain time in the world, but it became one of the most memorable chapters of my life. My daughter Cassi, who was working in football operations, was on staff with us. Every day, I got to go to work with her, and when everything shut down, my son Jackson came out and lived with us for four months. He's now the special teams coordinator at Marshall University, but during that time, we were all together again. It was a season of togetherness I'll never forget.

These days, I'm at Bowling Green. I'm four years strong, and we've had three straight bowl games. I spent the first few years with an incredibly loyal friend, Coach Scot Loeffler, and now I'm working with Eddie George, a guy who understands greatness and leadership at the highest level. Both have been fantastic to me. We've built strong teams, forged real locker room cultures, and we're still chasing that magic—still pushing for championships.

Through every chapter—Notre Dame, Wisconsin, Florida, Boston College, Colorado, Bowling Green—what's mattered most hasn't been the win-loss record or the headlines. It's been the people. I got the chance to walk into locker rooms filled with talented young men and help shape who they're becoming on and off the field.

WHY THE LOCKER ROOM IS NOT FOR SALE

If you want to understand why I say the locker room is not for sale, you have to understand where I come from. Like I said, I was raised in a locker room. I grew up in that space because my dad was a coach. The locker room taught me what it means to be part of something bigger than yourself, and I've spent my entire career defending that space.

When I was coaching at Wisconsin, people were always trying to get close to the program. We were winning big games, playing on national TV in packed stadiums. That drew attention, and friends and colleagues from all over wanted tickets. I get it, of course. People want to experience the tradition and the pageantry of college football, especially with a winning team.

I had a buddy from my Fordham days who worked with me back when I was on Wall Street at Drexel Burnham. That was the big-time junk bond firm, the one that helped finance the rise of Las Vegas and those massive hotels like the Mirage. During our Rose Bowl run, my buddy called me up and said, "Can you get me ten tickets?"

I said, "Sure."

Then he asked, "Can I get a couple sideline passes?"

Again, I said yes, but then he asked one more thing. He said, "If you win, can I bring my clients into the locker room after the game?"

I didn't even hesitate. I said, "Absolutely not."

See, the locker room isn't entertainment. It's not part of the hospitality package. It's not a bonus for VIPs or a backdrop for photo ops.

The locker room belongs only to the players and coaches who put in the blood, sweat, and sacrifice to earn their place inside it. You don't compromise that—not for anyone.

The foundation of the locker room is trust. If you violate that trust, you break something that can't be bought back. What happens in that room—the emotions, the speeches, the silence before a game, the tears after a loss, the celebration after a win—that belongs to the team. It's personal and private.

People always say, "There's no *I* in team." Well, there's no *I* in *trust* either, but there is an "us." And *us* is what you're trying to build in a locker room. It's not just a collection of talent or a roster you're putting together. No, the locker room is a real, unified, bonded group of young men who trust each other with everything. That starts with putting "we" before "me" and "us" before "I." That mindset changes a team, and it only happens when the space they share is protected, respected, and never sold.

The locker room is a way of life, and once you've truly been a part of it—once you've felt what it means to belong to something that real—you'll fight to preserve it, too.

WHERE TRUST IS EARNED

People ask me all the time what I love most about coaching. Is it the big wins? The bowl games? Coaching a Heisman Trophy winner? All of those moments are special, and I've had the privilege of standing on the sideline during some of the biggest games in college football. I've watched Ron Dayne carry an entire stadium on his back. I've seen championships won and dreams realized, but that's not what means the most to me.

What I loved most—and what I'll never stop loving—is walking into the locker room in the middle of the week. There's usually music blasting, players dancing, laughing, and messing around. The energy is electric. That's the heartbeat of the team. That's where the real stuff is happening. Friendships are being built, and trust is being earned. You get to know your guys in that space, in those little moments between the grind. That's where you see who they are and who they're becoming.

Ask any former coach or player, and they'll tell you the locker room is what they miss the most. It's not the touchdowns or even the championships. What stays deeply rooted in your soul is the time in the locker room, where you experience the camaraderie and the inside jokes, the pregame nerves and the postgame joy. It's the shared experience of growing up together, shoulder to shoulder, through every high and low.

That's what makes it irreplaceable. For young people, especially in college, the locker room is far more than a place where they change clothes. It's where the anxieties of becoming adults are met with support, laughter, and brotherhood. It's where the pressure lets up and the heart opens up. That space has solved more problems than any lecture hall ever could.

And the celebration there is on a whole other level. You can't manufacture that kind of spontaneous, gut-level joy. It's intoxicating. It's primal and honest. The locker room after a win feels like everything good in the world just exploded in one room. No boardroom, no bonus check, no corporate rally will ever recreate that. Believe me: they've tried.

I've got a good friend, David Chao, who spent his career as a trader on Wall Street. He told me recently, "We've always tried to recreate the locker room here." You've probably seen the energy and excitement on the trading floor. It's not an accident. The guys running those firms know there's power in brotherhood, in shared wins and losses, in the raw emotion of chasing victory together.

I spent two years on Wall Street. I was there when the market crashed in 1987, and I'll tell you from experience, as intense and fascinating as it was, it wasn't the same. The locker room is different. The celebrations there are authentic in a way the world can't duplicate. You're not cheering because your portfolio grew. You're cheering because your people grew, because the guy next to you fought like hell and came out the other side better. Every win feels personal, and every loss is shared.

Captain Brock Horne celebrating a great win and the pure joy expressed after a win a
(Photo © Bowling Green State University Athletics—Owen Fink)

Eddie George and his team celebrating a win over rival Toledo in the locker room
(Photo © Bowling Green State Athletics—Avery Zeurcher)

You can't replicate that with quarterly earnings or performance reviews. That's why we keep coming back to it. That's why former players call me years later and say, "Coach, I miss the locker room." That's the fix they're after.

It's where we become more than athletes. It's where we become brothers. And as we'll explore in the coming pages, it has so much to teach us about how to be effective coaches, teachers, parents, and leaders. That's why, no matter what the world offers, no matter how tempting the outside access may seem, the locker room is not for sale.

CHAPTER ONE

THE HUMAN TOUCH ALWAYS WINS

WHAT DOES THE locker room represent? To me, it's the best of America in a single room. *E pluribus unum*—out of many, one. You walk through those doors and the labels fall off fast: race, religion, hometown, class year. Freshman or senior, starter or scout team, it doesn't matter. The locker room is a crucible of heat and pressure that melts differences and forges a team.

That's the beauty of this place and of team sports. People from every background learn to move in the same direction, toward a shared purpose. The walls that divide us outside don't stand a chance here. We listen, we work, we sweat, we hold each other accountable, and we become something bigger than ourselves. That's the goal every day—out of many, one.

I was raised in a house where the scoreboard mattered, but people mattered more. My dad, Don White, was a football coach and high school economics teacher. He gave definition to the word *swagger* well before Joe Namath ever thought of putting on his array of mink coats.

My mom, Maureen White, was an English teacher who kidnapped energy and released it to freedom every day in her classroom. Between the two of them, I learned the simplest, hardest truth in this business: if you want to coach well, you have to love well. You don't reach players from a whiteboard. You reach them by earning the right to be heard day after day until trust is the foundation under every drill, meeting, and hard conversation.

That conviction got sharpened at Notre Dame under Joe Moore, the legendary offensive line coach whose name sits on the award given to the best line in the country. Joe was tough as boot leather, and his players adored him. One afternoon, when I was a twenty-three-year-old assistant, he leaned in and said, "You want to be a great coach? Feed 'em."

He wasn't being cute. He meant it literally. If you feed them, you can coach them hard because they know you care. The quickest way to a player's heart might be through a plate of spaghetti, but the real point is presence. Let them see you as a husband, a dad, a human being who burns burgers on the grill sometimes. When they see that, the whistle on your neck sounds different. It sounds like someone who's *for* them. There is no doubt that "coaching outside the lines without a whistle" is just as important as "coaching inside the lines with a whistle." This is why the human touch always wins and is so vital to coaching today.

I watched my father live that way. The guys he coached as high-schoolers—Dante Muzzioli, Joe Finnegan, Dave Ramsey, Tom Cassidy, Joe Habelow, Lou Bruno, Bobby Shea, Peter Sullivan and plenty more—were fixtures at our little lake place in the summers. I was six or seven, running around wide-eyed while those "giants" threw a football on the beach and ate my dad's array of specialty Italian sausages, gourmet burgers, perfectly barbecued chicken, and mouth-watering steak tips marinated to perfection. Fifty-plus years later, those relationships still hold up. That is not an accident. That's the dividend of a coach who stayed present in their lives long after the two-a-days ended.

That's why I say "relationships first, football second." When you've broken bread with a player, you've earned the right to correct him. When he's seen you hold your own kids accountable, he understands why you're holding him to a standard. When the relationship is real, the tough talk isn't personal but purposeful. We can demand with love, and compete without losing who we are.

The human touch always wins. Schemes evolve, terminology changes, and trends come and go, but trust is undefeated. Build that, and the locker room becomes something money can't buy and pressure can't break. That's the team I want. That's the team I'll spend my life coaching.

You know the human touch always wins when your quarterback, Brooks Bollinger from the Wisconsin Badgers, is babysitting with his then girlfriend Natalie and now wife and teaches your daughter Cassi how to tie her shoes with the "bunny ears" technique. I will remember Brooks more for this memory shot than any of his Wisconsin Hall of Fame heroics on the field. That's why the human touch always wins. It penetrates. It permeates. It produces permanent memories of moments to be captured.

THE HARDEST CALLS

Let me take you back to 1974. My dad had rebuilt a struggling program at Belmont High School in Massachusetts, and they were rolling—8–0 at one point, finishing 8–2. It was the best team the school had seen in years, and he was facing a brutal decision at quarterback. On one side was respected senior, Paul Bounty, who was a natural leader and a returning starter who had earned every ounce of trust in that locker room. On the other was a junior, Joey Saia, a gunslinger who could spin it like Joe Namath and stretch the field like no one else.

I was ten years old, riding home from practices with my dad, listening to him talk. It was clear he loved Paul. Everyone did. But he also knew what the team needed to reach its ceiling that year. When he finally chose Joey to start and asked Paul to back him up, it hurt. It was hard, but the moment the decision was made, with a lot of honesty and respect, there was a sense of freedom. The team had clarity because the roles were defined, and Paul, because he was a real leader, kept leading and found ways to contribute to this unforgettable season.

Decades later, I found myself at Wisconsin in the same kind of moment. Ron Dayne was a freshman with legs like tree trunks and a burst that made the field feel shorter. Our junior captain, Carl McCullough, is one of the finest men I've coached. He's reliable, selfless, and beloved by his teammates. Ron had a breakout game against Stanford, and the next week, I sat down with Carl and told him Ron would start. He asked me why, and I gave him the plain truth: "If I need one yard with my life on the line, I'm handing the ball to Ron." That wasn't a knock on Carl. It was simply a commitment to our purpose, because I had watched my father do the hard, right thing years before, I knew how to do it with compassion and respect.

Real teams are built on relationships strong enough to endure hard conversations. When trust is the foundation, you can make the call that serves the whole, even when it disappoints someone you care about. Those conversations are never easy, but they're necessary. And when you have them the right way, resentment gives way to resolve, and confusion gives way to commitment.

That's coaching. That's leadership in general. You don't avoid the hard call. Rather, you earn the right to make it, and then make it for the good of the team.

"FEED THEM"—WHY IT WORKS

Joe Moore told me something that has motivated my approach for four decades now: "Feed them, and you can coach them hard." When a player sits at your kitchen table, when he sees your home, meets your wife, hears your kids laughing down the hall, he sees you as a whole person, not just a whistle and a practice script. That kind of proximity builds trust fast, and trust is the only foundation strong enough to hold tough conversations and high standards.

Hospitality lowers defenses. A plate of food does what a thousand speeches can't because it says, "You matter here." Players talk differently over burgers than they do under stadium lights. They open up about classes, family, fear, and dreams. You learn who needs a push and who needs a hand. Then, when it's time to raise the bar, they know the edge of your voice is backed by the weight of your care.

I've carried that idea everywhere I've coached. My wife, Salli, is the real hero of it all. She welcomes the boys like sons, and the house fills up with the comforting smells of steaks on the grill, burgers popping, and those Thursday chocolate chip cookies that have become as dependable as game tape. We've made ice cream sandwiches in August heat, set extra plates at Thanksgiving, and found room for one more chair more times than I can count. Ask the men I've coached what made the biggest impact, and they'll mention two things: the energy I bring to the field and the food we served around our table.

Meals create connection because they create comfort. When a young man walks into our home, drops his backpack by the door, and smells something on the grill, he exhales. The shoulders come down. The jokes start. You learn more in fifteen minutes around a kitchen island than you do in a week of position meetings, because people are themselves when they feel at home. You're creating an environment where they don't have to perform; they just get to be.

We've tried to make our house open, warm, and easy to be in. We want an atmosphere where the players feel comfortable laughing over the sizzle of burgers and sharing stories between bites. It's simple, and that's why it works. When a player sees you "apron-on" instead of "whistle-on," he learns who you are, and when he knows who you are, he can trust what you're asking him to become.

The guys love coming over. They'll tell you that themselves. They know they're welcome, they know they're safe, and they know we're glad they're here. Comfort turns into conversation, conversation turns into honesty, and honesty turns into accountability. That's the progression. You don't earn the right to coach a player hard until you've earned the right to know him well.

Coach Moore and his belief in "feeding 'em" confirmed what my dad modeled as he fed his high school team. My dad loved to cook and learned Italian cooking from the mother of one of his players. In 1972, the foundation of "Cooking with Coach" was poured when Michael Manfredi's mom taught my dad to make a "Sunday sauce" (or "gravy") to die for, meatballs so moist and otherworldly, and eggplant Parmesan that still ruins restaurant versions for me. I still have the handwritten recipes from 1972—over fifty years ago.

One of the most memorable Sundays of my life was February 24, 2019, when my college teammate and dear friend Frank Ciota's wonderful mom, Margaret, taught me her tricks for sauce and meatballs. We called it the Feast of San Ciota, and it's a day I'll always cherish. Football and the power of the locker room made this happen thirty-six years after our last down together. That's brotherhood at its best; the locker room truly stands the test of time.

Finally, at Colorado State, wide receiver Thomas Pannunzio and his parents, Carol and Nick, made homemade ravioli every week and shared family recipes that are, quite simply, unforgettable.

Feeding your team then isn't a gimmick. Break bread, build trust, tell the truth, demand their best, and love them through it. That's how you turn a roster into a family, and a family into a team that can handle hard coaching and win the right way.

CONNECTION BEATS PEDIGREE

People ask me all the time how to win in recruiting. How do you walk into a living room without a blue-blood logo on your chest and walk out with a commitment? My answer is always the same: connection beats pedigree. Parents and players aren't buying a brand. They're judging a person. They're asking, "Will this coach be there for my son when the lights are off?"

My first real proof of that came at UNLV. I was twenty-five, recruiting Demond Thompkins, a gifted receiver from Eisenhower High in Rialto, California. The Pac-12 was in his living room. A former NFL star was on him. On paper, I didn't belong in the race, so I did the one thing I could do: I showed up. Every week, I was there at school, at the house, on the field. After class, we'd throw the ball around with his buddies, run a little flag football, laugh, compete, and talk about life. I learned

Demond Thompkins, Jason Davis, Brian White, and Omar Love—The Ike Mob
(Photo © Salli White)

his parents' hopes, not just his forty times. In the end, that young man chose UNLV over the bigger and shinier names. I didn't have the bigger resume, but I built a stronger relationship.

Many more players from this celebrated high school would follow Demond to UNLV. They were known as the "Ike Mob." This is how recruiting goes: get one ,and others will follow.

Years later, at Boston College, I met a wiry, under recruited receiver from University School in Fort Lauderdale named Zay Flowers. Five-nine, a buck-fifty, overlooked by almost everyone, his high school coach, Daniel Luque, kept saying, "Coach, when the game's on the line, I put the ball in his hands."

I believed him. I believed the kid. I went to practices, sat with his family, and realized he was something special. He came in and scored in the first game of his career. He kept scoring and grew into a first-round draft pick of the Baltimore Ravens and a pro who plays the game with joy. The point is, talent is real, but belief is rocket fuel. Sometimes the relentless care unlocks what the rankings can't see.

Then there's A. J. Dillon. When I took over the running backs at Boston College, our staff changes immediately impacted the recruiting of A. J. for the worse. My first school visit with him didn't really receive rave reviews; in fact, it was quite the opposite. Word came back, "Coach, he's not feeling it." Still, I didn't get defensive. I asked him for one simple shot: "Let me coach you at camp for three days. If you don't like how I coach you, I'll tip my cap and move on."

He agreed. He came to camp, and we worked and sweated, but we also talked about more than football. By the end, he chose Boston College and became the school's all-time leading rusher. Now he's punishing tacklers on Sundays. That turnaround didn't happen because I delivered a fancy pitch. It happened because I listened, stayed present, and let the coaching speak for itself. Salli and I even got invited to his wedding, and she made him an extra special batch of her famous cookies that A. J. used to devour.

*Salli and A. J. with a batch of her famous chocolate chip
cookies, prewedding*

That's the throughline in every recruiting win I've ever had: consistency. Show up when the cameras aren't there. Learn about the family, be honest about where the young man stands and what it will take for him to grow. Feed him, figuratively and literally, and then coach him hard because he knows you care. Parents and players both feel that. Logos can dazzle for a night, but trust is what carries a four-year relationship, and many times, true friendships that last forever.

Like clockwork, I can count on a telephone call at 6:00 a.m. from Leo Boese, the father of Joey, on my birthday. Recruitment turns into friendship turns into family. I know I can count on Leo Boese and his family to always be there for me and my family. This is the immense power of the human touch. It penetrates the superficial skin level and hangs out forever in the veins and flows fluently through the arteries as the blood that promotes brotherhood. This is powerful and real and we all now know real is rare, and real has no color.

One of the joys of coaching is connecting with a family during recruiting and watching them truly become family to you. The Ciaffoni family is that family. I recruited Mike to Boston College, and we soon became part of their family, and they became part of ours. Dad, Joe, became a daily early-morning telephone conversation for wisdom and leadership nuggets. Mom, Sue, stuffed players, my dad, and me with insane meals on Sundays. I quickly got over the fact that she was a Yankees fanatic when she made this to-die-for strawberry shortcake for my birthday. Younger brother Nick soon became my biggest fan on any social media platform, and sisters Emma and Bella were a blast to watch grow up in real time. Mike, Nick, Joe and I still critique pizzerias from all over the country and quickly contact each other when we find a new one to add to the list.

Another is when a former player decides to coach because his experience was so good that he wants "perpetual recess" as a calling. Eddie Faulkner and his family check both boxes. Eddie was a running back for me at Wisconsin—a very good one—sandwiched between Ron Dayne and Michael Bennett, both first-round draft picks. Recruiting Eddie and his family was a blast. They had personality to spare, and on Christmas Eve 1995, Salli and I made a home visit to Muncie, Indiana (yes, it was legal then to recruit on Christmas Eve). He made my Christmas by committing to be a Badger later that night as we were driving home. Eddie gave the NFL a shot, then quickly pursued his passion for coaching, and is now the running backs coach for the Pittsburgh Steelers.

I'm very proud of Eddie and his accomplishments, but even prouder that he coaches with incredible passion and, every year, gives back to the Muncie community through his Team Faulk camp, which he runs with his family. I had the privilege of coaching at the camp this past June, and it filled me with pride to participate and watch Eddie and his family bring the "human touch" to Muncie.

The locker room isn't for sale. It's earned in kitchens and guidance offices, on practice fields after the bell rings, in the quiet moments when a family is choosing a program and the person behind it. Connection beats pedigree every time.

CHAPTER TWO

THE VALUES OF THE LOCKER ROOM

THE LOCKER ROOM is a crucible. You walk in as a bunch of individuals, and under heat and pressure, you come out as a team. Here, the temperature is set by the guys next to you. You learn fast, because your brothers won't let you stay the same.

Discipline and accountability are the values on display. They start with something as simple as how the room looks. You've got clean lockers, gear where it belongs, and tape in the bin. This matters because if we can't take care of the square foot right in front of us, how are we going to take care of third and two with the game on the line? I've seen great teams long before I saw them play just by walking through their locker room. Our legendary equipment man at UNLV, Paul Pucciarelli, used to say, "There's a direct line between a tidy locker room and a tidy game." Can you follow simple instructions? Can you focus on simple tasks every day?

The room tells the truth. It's a daily report card on what the head coach values and what the team is willing to live up to. The uniform

Paul "Pooch" Pucciarelli, legendary UNLV Director of Athletic Equipment, 2024 UNLV Athletic Hall of Fame Inductee, and Emeritus Member of the UNLV Faculty Staff (Photo © UNLV Photo Services)

of a team also speaks volumes about the values of a team and the head coach. As "Pooch" so eloquently states, "It's a *uni*-form, meaning 'one form,' not a hundred different interpretations. It's a uniform, not a costume. It's not Halloween."

There's also a natural hierarchy here. The seniors teach the juniors, who teach the sophomores, who teach the freshmen. Standards cascade downward. You don't keep the room squared away for the coach. You do it for the guy beside you, because you're going to battle with him in two hours. That's accountability. You don't hide in a mess. You stand in order and say, "You can count on me."

Toughness grows in that same soil. I'm talking about the kind of toughness that keeps fighting hard on the field even when nobody's clapping. When you're sore, it's the toughness that stacks the pads. When you have a bad practice, you own it, fix it, and help the next man not repeat it. That's how toughness turns into teamwork. It's individual pride channeled toward a shared purpose.

Selflessness is the heartbeat. You put your ego on the top shelf with your helmet, and you pick up someone else's slack before the coaches ever see it. You'll never convince me you can be a "me-first" player in a "we-first" room. The culture spits that out. You learn to celebrate the guard's down block as loudly as the receiver's touchdown because you understand both are part of the same sentence.

Community is built in the mundane acts like taping ankles, sharing scout notes, and sweeping up after. We break bread, we break down film, we break a sweat. Over time, those shared, ordinary reps turn into something extraordinary: brotherhood. And that brotherhood is what lets you chase competitive greatness. It's the standard of performing your very best when your very best is required. You don't rise to the occasion. You rise to your training, and the room is where that training starts.

Everything in the locker room runs on one power source: respect. Respect for the game. Respect for the work. Respect for each other. It shows up in how you talk to a trainer, how you listen to a GA, how you treat the walk-on who just earned his spot. It's also how you handle yourself when nobody's watching, because the locker room always is.

In our program, respect is the spine of how we operate. Keep that air clean and that spine strong, and you give yourself a chance to play championship football when the pressure gets intense.

If you step inside the locker room of a winning team and look around, you'll see respect in every label facing out, every helmet lined just so, every veteran showing a freshman how we do things. That's a culture of respect, and culture wins.

THE FOUR WALLS OF THE LOCKER ROOM

Discipline is the first lesson of the locker room, and accountability is the second—so close behind you can't tell them apart. Every day, I ask my players one simple question: "Can I count on you? Can I count on you not when the cameras are on, not when the crowd is loud—can I count on you on Tuesday after a hard lift, on Thursday when your legs are sore, on Saturday when it's fourth and inches?" That's the measure. Discipline sets the standard, and accountability proves it.

I tell our guys there are four walls and a floor to every great locker room. The walls are *respect, trust, love,* and *commitment.* The floor, the thing everything stands on, is *brotherhood.* If those walls aren't straight and that floor isn't solid, the room collapses. But if they're strong, you can build a championship culture inside them.

It all starts with respect. Players respect toughness, they respect accountability, they respect honesty, and they respect hard work. They admire talent, of course, but they respect the grind. Respect shows up when you're five deep in the depth chart and still take notes like a starter. Respect is earned daily, not awarded on signing day.

Trust is the next wall. Trust answers the question, "Can I count on you?" It's built rep by rep, meeting by meeting, sprint by sprint. It's not flashy. It's not a tweet. It's a thousand quiet yeses to the team's standards: be on time, know your assignment, finish your block, help your brother.

Love is the toughest word in football, but it lives in every great room. Love is serving your teammate when there's nothing in it for you. It's giving up reps to get a freshman ready, picking up pads that aren't yours, owning your mistake before the film does. Love turns "me" into "we."

Commitment seals it. Commitment is not feeling. It's a decision. It's doing the right thing long after the mood you made the promise in has gone away. It's boring, consistent, relentless follow-through. Commitment has no conditions. You are either all in or all out. No prenups here. Proud to be a Falcon, a Ram, an Eagle, a Gator, a Badger from sunup to sundown and committed to being the best I can possibly be.

And the floor of the locker room is brotherhood. We create blood in this room, a bond that outlives seasons and scoreboards. Brotherhood is the reason you strain for one more inch when no one would blame you for coming up short. It's why you run toward the pressure, not away from it.

Now, the locker room is hierarchical. Seniors to juniors to sophomores to freshmen—that's the pecking order, but once you get past age, productivity and trust take over. Can you play? Are you prepared? Will you show up when the chips are down? I use the dark-alley test: if it's 2:00 a.m. and trouble finds me, do I want you with me? The locker room answers that question quickly. It finds the men you can trust and exposes the ones you can't. That's the beauty of it. There's nowhere to hide. Frauds get sorted out by Tuesday. Fakes don't make it through winter workouts.

So, yes, discipline and accountability are where we start, but the goal is bigger. Build the four walls, lay the brotherhood floor, and then live, fight, and play like it matters. Be someone your teammates respect, someone they trust, someone they know is committed, someone who loves this team enough to put his ego on the shelf. Do that, and the locker room will shape your season and your life.

This is why Head Coach Steve Addazio placed such a premium on discipline and accountability within the locker room, entrusting his most loyal lieutenant and lifelong consigliere, Frank Leonard, with the daily inspections. To bring some creativity and personality to these inspections, we launched #LeonardsLockers, a series where I interviewed Coach Leonard as he graded the players' lockers. What started as a simple idea quickly became a social media sensation. Parents and players alike tuned in every week to watch each new episode. Coach Leonard's colorful commentary—and the occasional guest appearance by his young daughters, Maria and Sara—turned the series into must-watch content, offering a blend of insight, humor, and heart that resonated far beyond the locker room.

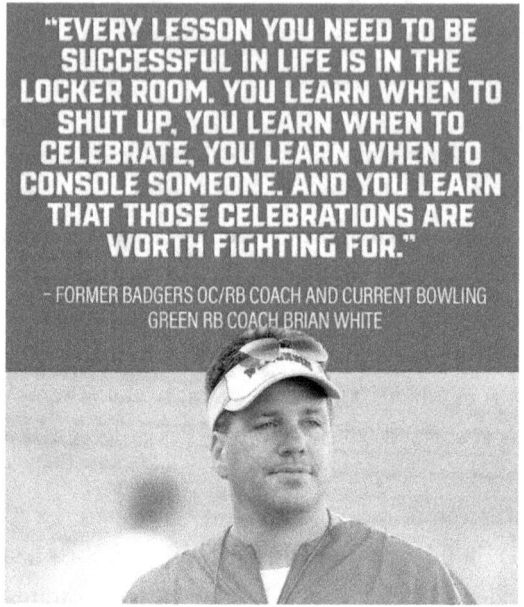

"EVERY LESSON YOU NEED TO BE SUCCESSFUL IN LIFE IS IN THE LOCKER ROOM. YOU LEARN WHEN TO SHUT UP. YOU LEARN WHEN TO CELEBRATE. YOU LEARN WHEN TO CONSOLE SOMEONE. AND YOU LEARN THAT THOSE CELEBRATIONS ARE WORTH FIGHTING FOR."

– FORMER BADGERS OC/RB COACH AND CURRENT BOWLING GREEN RB COACH BRIAN WHITE

EARN THE LOCKER

New England Patriots 2025 first-round draft pick, OT–Will Campbell said it perfectly: "The money can wait. First, earn the locker room."

That line tells me everything I need to know about a young man's compass. It says he was raised right, in a real locker room, with real standards. Here, respect isn't handed out with a jersey. It's earned, day by day, by how you work, how you listen, and how you commit even when the game's not going well. Commercials and NIL deals can chase you later. First, prove you belong to your brothers.

The locker room is your first proving ground. Before you ever see a live snap, the older guys are watching. Can you do your job? Will you work hard? Are you good people when the game gets hard and the lights go off? We're not hunting for perfect people. We're hunting for dependable men who raise the standard. You gain respect here the old-fashioned way, by being on time, knowing your assignment, finishing, and helping the next man. Rookies don't need smart slogans. They need winning habits.

Trust is the currency, and trust is gained by keeping your word. In 1998, at Wisconsin, the players came to me during camp with a challenge: "Coach, if we're undefeated going into Michigan, you've got to do something special."

I said, "Deal. If we're undefeated, you can shave my head—right after we beat Minnesota for the Axe."

They laughed. I laughed. Then we kept winning. Week by week, that promise became part of our story. On game day against Minnesota, Eddie Faulkner looked me in the eye and said, "Coach, you're going to be bald tonight."

We took care of business, and before the Gatorade dried, Chris McIntosh and a herd of linemen carried me into the locker room, where the clippers were already humming. They shaved me clean on the spot. Maybe it was silly, but it was absolutely important that I kept my word and they kept theirs. That's how a team's spine gets stronger, by keeping your word and honoring your promises.

Respect also looks like a freshman walking in with his mouth shut and his work turned up. Ron Dayne was that guy. He was highly touted, but he didn't posture or preen. He went to work. The seniors could see that this kid would help us win. In a heartbeat, the hierarchy flipped from age to productivity. That's the rule in every great room. Once you've shown you can be counted on, you're in. If you're selfish or self-absorbed, the culture will spit you out by Tuesday. Ron wasn't. He earned it the right way through quiet effort, consistent results, and a team-first mentality, and the room embraced him.

That's why Will Campbell's mindset matters. Talent gets you through the door, but respect keeps you in the room. You don't chase the spotlight; you chase the standard. Earn your brothers' trust, and the rest has a way of finding you. The money can wait. The commercials can wait. Your character cannot.

So here's the lesson I give every young player: make the locker room your first audience. Let your actions speak. Keep your word. Do your job. Serve the team. When the chips are down and it's fourth and inches on the field or in life, be the man they point to and say, "I want him in my foxhole."

DISMANTLING THE "ISMS" OF THE WORLD

The locker room takes the isms of the world (racism, sexism, ageism, all of them) and grinds them down into brotherhood, sisterhood, motherhood, fatherhood, servanthood, and neighborhoods. I tell our guys all the time, "*ISM* might as well stand for 'I, self, and me.'" That's the world's language. Everyone's looking out for number one. But in the locker room, the language is "we" and "us." Out there, people build walls. In here, we take the walls down because the room is too intimate for pretense. You dress next to a man, sweat next to him, lift with him, win and lose with him, sooner or later you learn his story, and when you know his story, it's hard to throw up a label and walk away.

Peer pressure is the engine that drives this. Every group has forms of peer pressure, whether teams, companies, or families, but the locker room turns it into a force for good. The standard becomes contagious. If you want to be accepted, uphold the standard. Show respect, do your job, and keep your word. In this environment, the posturing dries up fast because the room sorts it out. The locker room has a way of revealing who's real and who's just rehearsing.

Football helps because it's a meritocratic game to its core. The best players play. Coaches who don't put the best on the field get fired. That reality cuts through a lot of nonsense and posturing. Freshman or senior, Black or white, city kid or farm kid, if you can help us win and you live our values, the room is going to embrace you. If you can't, or you won't, the room will move on without you. It's not cruel; it's honest.

I've seen that kind of honesty forge beautiful friendships. A couple of seasons back, our National Special Teams Player of the Year—PaSean Wimberly, a Black student from Toledo already working on a master's in architecture—bonded with a white walk-on running back, Bryce DeFalco, from Pemberville, a small town near Bowling Green. They came from very different backgrounds, but the locker room brought them together. They became roommates, and recently Bryce's family took PaSean to Mexico to celebrate Bryce's twenty-first birthday. That's family, forged in the locker room by shared work and shared standards.

Dr. Martin Luther King taught that division grows when people don't know one another. The locker room forces that knowledge. You talk to each other. You listen to each other and see. You learn the why behind a teammate's habits, the sacrifices his family made, maybe even the chip on his shoulder. Fear doesn't hold up well under that kind of light. Neither do stereotypes. Respect takes their places.

The locker room merged the Wimberly and DeFalco families as they celebrate Senior Day in Doyt Perry Stadium (Photo © Danielle DeFalco)

*PaSean Wimberly and Bryce Defalco—a brotherhood
for life forged through the locker room
(Photo © Danielle DeFalco)*

I don't care what box the world puts you in, whether religion, race, or age, if you can play, prepare, and be counted on, you're ours. I've coached rooms where a freshman walked in and took a job because he earned it. The seniors didn't resent it. On the contrary, they respected it. That's how a healthy culture works. We honor the hierarchy for teaching, but we honor productivity for playing.

That's the beauty of the locker room. It doesn't pretend that the isms don't exist. Instead, it starves them. It replaces "I, self, me" with "we, us, team." It turns strangers into brothers and teammates into the kind of neighbors you'd trust to watch your house, help your family, or pull you through when life goes third and long.

A BLUEPRINT WORTH COPYING

If more leaders studied what happens in a good locker room—really studied it—they would see a blueprint worth copying. They would see shared standards, earned respect, truth-telling, and love expressed as service. That's how the walls come down. That's how a room becomes a brotherhood, and that's why, in our program, the locker room is not for sale.

Why do the values of the locker room matter beyond football? Because they outlast the jersey. The lessons don't stop at graduation. A great locker room is transformational, not transactional. Transactions end when the clock hits zero. Transformation keeps working on you in the office, at the dinner table, in your community, long after the stadium lights go dark.

I'm nearly four decades removed from my college locker room, and those relationships are still rock solid. We don't talk about scores anymore. These days, we talk about children, surgeries, job changes, setbacks, personal and professional victories, yet it's the same bond. That bond was built the same way, through discipline, accountability, trust, love, and commitment, standing on the floor of brotherhood. Time hasn't weakened it. Time has proven it because the ceiling of the locker room is *forever*! This is truly the priceless gift that the locker room keeps giving: a brotherhood that lasts a lifetime. It's real, it's rare, and it has *no color*!

The values hold up because life keeps asking the same questions the game asked: Can I count on you? Will you show up when it's inconvenient? Do you tell the truth even when it costs you? Will you put the team (your family, your coworkers, your community) ahead of your ego? Football was just the rehearsal, but real life is the game.

In business, discipline looks like doing the boring right thing over and over again without applause. Accountability looks like owning the miss in the 8:00 a.m. meeting before the spreadsheet forces you to do it. Trust sounds like saying, "I've got it," and then actually having it. Love shows up as service, maybe staying late so a teammate can get home, or making the tough call because it's best for the whole. Commitment is showing up on the hard Tuesdays of life, not just the trophy Saturdays.

That's why the locker room is not for sale. You can't buy these values, and you can't fake them for long. You earn them, daily, shoulder to shoulder with people who expect your best and give you theirs. Do that faithfully, and the reward is bigger than a season banner. The real reward is a life marked by strong relationships and a reputation that stands the test of time.

The values of the locker room matter far beyond sports. They build marriages, raise children, lead teams, and heal neighborhoods. They turn strangers into brothers and seasons into lifelong friendships. The scoreboard changes, and the headlines fade. But the men you become, and the way you love, work, and serve, those are wins that last.

CHAPTER THREE

MOTIVATION IS EVERYWHERE

MOTIVATION IS EVERYWHERE if you're paying attention. You can find it painted on cinderblock walls, taped to lockers, stenciled down a hallway. Some of the best coaching I've ever seen is written in six-inch letters where teenagers walk to first period.

I collect these bits of wisdom like treasures as I go through my day. I saw a mural painted on a slab of concrete with pull-up bars attached at Crenshaw High in South Central Los Angeles, with a line from four-time Gold Medalist Olympian, Jesse Owens: "The battles that count aren't the ones for gold medals. The struggles within yourself—the invisible, inevitable battles inside all of us—that's where it's at."

That's not just a poetic line. That's a game plan for life. In this era, mental health is more important than ever, and the locker room's job is to help young people win those invisible, inevitable battles with anxiety, doubt, fatigue, or the thousand tiny things that pile up between sunrise and lights out.

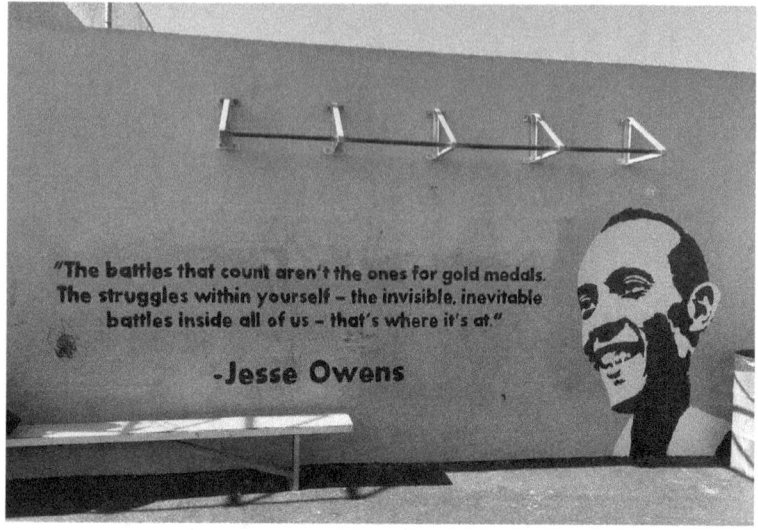

Jesse Owens quote at Crenshaw High School in Los Angeles (Photo © Brian White)

Down another hallway, I saw a poster that read, "It's nice to be important, but it's more important to be nice." It's simple and true. The corridor was spotless, which told me everything about the culture. That's the human touch beating the tough-guy act. You don't have to bully your way through high school or through a team. Live the golden rule. Say please and thank you. Pick up the tape you didn't drop. The room remembers who you are when no one's watching.

That's why these hallway lines matter. They take big ideas and put them where you can't ignore them. Words on the wall become habits in the room: show up, do the work, tell the truth, serve your brother. Do that long enough, and those hallway quotes become your reflex under pressure.

At Northside High School in Georgia I saw a question painted big and bold: "What's your 68?" I asked the coach what it meant. He told me about Jaromir Jagr, the great Pittsburgh Penguin, who wore 68 to honor his grandfather and the year 1968—when the Soviets crushed Czechoslovakia's fight for freedom and his family paid the price. Jagr

Motivation is everywhere and all over high school hallways across the country
(Photo © Brian White)

High school hallways at Northside High School in Georgia (Photo © Brian White)

made his number a promise to never forget why you play and who you represent.

That question—*What's your 68?*—cuts straight to the heart. Today, people say, "What's your why?" It's the same idea. In our program, we ask every player to name it and live it. If you don't name your 68, you'll drift away slowly but surely.

Another day, I was driving through Pennsylvania with my family and an enormous Marine truck rolled by with a motto stretched across the trailer: "Earned. Never Given." I wanted to pull that slogan into our locker room because that's the standard. Jobs aren't given. Roles aren't given. Respect isn't given. You get what you earn, and you earn what you get. When a team decides to live like that, excellence wins.

I've also stood under a photo of Jackie Robinson with one word beneath it: Courage. He changed more than a sport—he changed a whole country—by meeting hatred with character and history with courage. That's competitive greatness in its purest form. Give your very best when your very best is required.

And then there are the giants whose lives preach louder than any slogan. During MLK week, schools fill halls with his words about dreams, and they should. However, Dr. King didn't just dream. He disciplined his life to match the dream. That's a blueprint for any team. Like Dr. King, align your habits with your vision.

SUNSETS AND BRIDGES

On the morning of our season opener in 2025, I took a walk from the incredible Hancock Hotel in Findlay and stopped at a plaque about the Underground Railroad. It called Findlay a "conductor haven" for fugitive slaves. I stood there thinking about the ordinary people who risked everything because they knew slavery was wrong and freedom was right. That kind of courage is costly. It's often done in the dark, with the door cracked and the lantern low, when the world isn't cheering. That's the same courage we try to grow in a locker room: do what's right, not what's easy; protect your brother even if it costs you.

Right next to that site was a bridge. Bridges are one of my favorite things. I take pictures of them everywhere I go. I love what they represent. Bridges connect what life tries to keep apart. They span the gap, and that's what great teams do. They connect locker rooms to neighborhoods, seniors to freshmen, talent to responsibility, vision to execution. A real program builds bridges between backgrounds and beliefs, between the man you are and the man you're becoming.

Motivation is everywhere if you're willing to look. Sometimes, it's etched in bronze, or painted on a wall, or rolling past on the side of a truck. The key is to find what *hits* you and let it shape your habits. I use quotes, photos, and stories with our players every day as teaching tools. A single image can get to the heart faster than a speech. That's why I stockpile pictures the way some coaches stockpile plays.

Sunrise in Boston and the Zakim Bridge (Photo © Brian White)

My favorite messages are the ones that come back to me. Former players and coaches will send a photo and a line—"Coach, saw this and thought of you." Frank Piraino, New England Patriots director of strength and conditioning, does it all the time. He knows I love sunrises and sunsets because they preach the same sermon twice a day: beginnings and endings, light after dark, rhythm and renewal. The sky reminds you to maintain perspective, to stack one faithful day on top of another. That's culture. That's brotherhood. That's how you build a life, not just a season.

So I tell our guys: be a bridge. Be courageous when no one is watching. Let the right words and the right images hold you to the standard. When the sun comes up—or goes down—take a breath, look around, and remember why we do this. The locker room is not for sale because what we're building can't be bought. It's earned, day by day, in small acts of courage that connect us to something bigger than ourselves.

KEEP YOUR EYES OPEN

If you want to spot inspiration in unexpected places and turn it into fuel, build a simple habit of capturing the moment. You won't always get a warning. Sometimes, inspiration will flash across your face at 7:13 a.m. on a Monday, and you either catch it or you miss it.

I learned that from my wife, Salli. Years ago at Wisconsin, Donnel Thompson and his brother Bryson were on the field together in the 1999 Rose Bowl. Salli had her Nikon—old-school film, not digital—and she snapped the only photo their family has of both boys playing at the same time: names on their backs, both taking on blocks like linebackers do. Decades later, Donnel texted me: "Coach, my dad still thanks you every time he looks at that picture." Salli captured the moment.

She also "captured the moment" on the last play of the Rose Bowl, Wendell Bryant sacked Cade McNown, and we won. Salli caught that too. Our sports information folks asked for the negative so they could

The Thompsom brothers playing together at the 1999 Rose Bowl
(Photo © Salli White)

make prints. Think about that. With one click, one frame, you've frozen a lesson you can teach for the next twenty-five years to finish, strain, and deliver when your very best is required.

So how do you practice "capturing the moment"? Be ready. Carry a notebook. Keep your camera handy. More importantly, keep your *eyes* open. Inspiration hides in plain sight. You may find it on a hallway wall or a street sign.

Slow down and see. It's easy to race past the good stuff. Salli and I drove our kids around this country between jobs, to state and national parks, Gettysburg, DC, the Pro Football Hall of Fame, New York City, the Grand Canyon, even the neon of Las Vegas. History isn't dusty when you stand in it. The places preach about courage, sacrifice, excellence, and your heart takes notes that your head can't forget.

Mount Rushmore and the beauty of
South Dakota (Photo © Brian White)

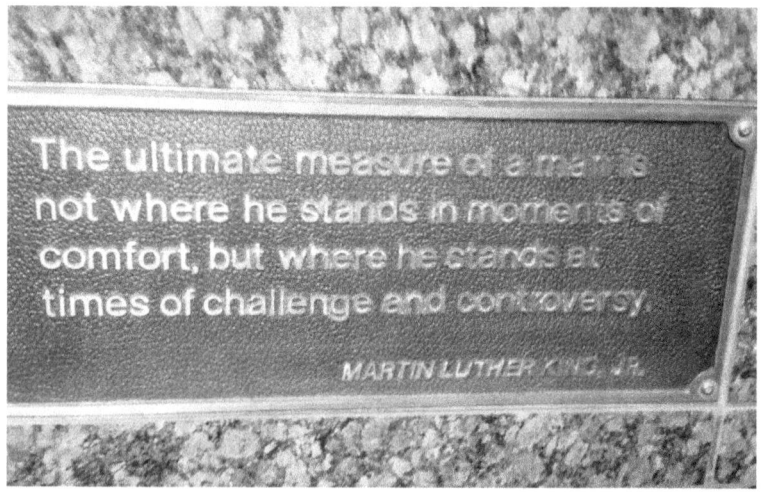

Famous quotes on the walls of the New York, New York Casino in Las Vegas
(Photo © Brian White)

Collect and share quotes, photos, little stories. Spot it, save it, and let it move you. Don't wait for the perfect speech or the perfect moment. Grab the lesson right in front of you and turn it into action. That's how you turn inspiration into fuel for the fire. You catch it, you keep it, and you use it to lift your standards today.

REMINDERS FOR PREPARATION

Small reminders drive big performance when they point you back to preparation. I love this definition of competitive excellence: *make the play when your number is called because you prepared to make it.* That moment on Saturday is earned on Tuesday and Wednesday through film study, walk-throughs, practice reps, and knowing your assignment cold. The reminder is a trigger that pulls the preparation to the surface right when you need it.

So we keep the cues simple and everywhere. In our locker room, the slogan on the wall is "Play hard. Play fast. Play long. Be a great teammate."

We say it in the meeting room. We tape it on the doorframe. Players write it on their wrist tape. We put it at the top of the scouting report. When the heat comes, a player may not rise to a speech, but they will default to their standards.

- **Play hard:** Put in the effort in every drill, every snap, with no off switch.
- **Play fast:** Clarity creates speed; when you know, you go.
- **Play long:** Stamina of mind and body; finish the fourth like you started the first.
- **Be a great teammate:** The human touch means encourage, communicate, and serve; make the guy next to you better.

Those are small reminders, but they add up to a big identity. When it's fourth and inches, you don't need a paragraph—you need a cue that unlocks all of that preparation. That's how little things become winning things. That's how a locker room turns standards into performance.

BUILDING A MOTIVATIONAL ENVIRONMENT

If you want to build a motivational environment as a coach, teacher, or parent, start by creating a space where people aren't intimidated. Make it positive, open, and uplifting. Let everyone speak. Let them try. Let them fail forward. Then flood that space with meaningful reminders, through words, images, and habits, that point them back to the standard every day. The dividend shows up when they start sending *you* the reminders back.

Wisconsin Head Coach Barry Alvarez masterfully built his championship program on the bricks and mortar of upbeat, positive motivation that always encouraged players to speak up and lead. Every year in January, Coach Alvarez gave the State of the Badger Address. This meeting reflected on the previous year and served as the beginning of building a new team from the ground up. The Cliff's Notes version confronted the disappointing ending to the 1997 season as the Georgia Bulldogs thoroughly defeated the Badgers 33–6 in the Outback Bowl, and it probably should have been much worse. After giving his thoughts, he opened the floor to any comments players wanted to express.

Junior Captain and current Wisconsin Athletics Director Chris McIntosh stood up and confidently said to his teammates, "I didn't come here to play in the Outback Bowl. I came here to play in and win the Rose Bowl."

I sat there stunned, thinking, *How crazy is that declaration? We just got thumped in the Outback Bowl and now we are going to win the Rose*

Ron Dayne and "Football Heaven" at the 1999 Rose Bowl
(Photo © Salli White)

Bowl? What unfolded was a magical, motivational, blueprint that led to two straight Rose Bowl wins in a row over UCLA and Stanford and Wisconsin being the first team in Big Ten history to win back-to-back Rose Bowls. An amazing tribute to a great locker room, positive leadership, and the human touch!

My core philosophy is simple: teach fundamentals and keep teaching them. I learned that from Lou Holtz. I call it the "constant conditioning of correct behavior." You don't hope people rise to the occasion; you train them to fall back on their training. That's why I'm known for one thing more than any other: ball security. I've got walls and binders full of photos that show it done right and wrong because pictures teach fast.

We call it *football heaven* and *football hell*.

1. **Heaven:** tip of the ball up, high and tight, "chin on the ball," elbow locked to the ribs—secure.
2. **Hell:** tip down, elbow flared off the cage—loose.

We post both. There's a Wall of Fame for the right technique and a Wall of Shame for the fix-it moments, and the Wall of Fame is always bigger. Celebrate what you want repeated. Correct what you want removed. Do both with clarity and respect.

The visuals work because they connect effort to identity. Years after Boston College, Jeff Smith—who played eight years in the NFL—texted me from Jets camp: "Coach, I know you'll love this—football heaven." He attached a shot of the ball high and tight, elbow welded in. That's the dividend. When your guys start coaching themselves—when they see the standard and feel proud to meet it—you've created a true motivational environment.

So how do you build one? Lower the fear, raise the standard. People perform best when they feel safe to speak and are pushed to grow. Make it clear: "We correct behaviors, not identities."

- Make the cues visible. Put the standards on the walls, in the playbook, on the wrist tape. Words become habits when they're seen and said daily.
- Teach with pictures. Show the exact posture, the exact foot, the exact finish. Let their eyes learn it before their muscles memorize it.
- Catch them doing it right. Expand the Wall of Fame. Shine a light on the behavior you want more of.
- Keep the joy high. Be upbeat and engaged, love what you do, and let them see you love it. Enthusiasm is a force multiplier.

In short, build a room where people can breathe easy, and then show them, over and over, what right looks like. The human touch wins. When you condition the correct behaviors and connect them to small, consistent reminders, those reminders turn into reflexes. Reflexes become standards. Standards become culture. And a culture built on clarity, care, and repetition produces big-time performance that lasts.

My parents taught me passion. Mom drilled this into me: *passion is caught, not taught.* What does that mean? People feel you before they remember you. Years from now, most players won't quote my speeches word for word, but they'll remember the energy in the room before kickoff, the lift after a tough loss, the way I coached with fire and joy.

If you asked the guys I've coached alongside or the players I've been blessed to coach, they would all say the same things: "He had energy, passion, loves coaching, loves developing young people. He's got energy that's infectious and worth imitating."

START WITH THE PERSON IN THE MIRROR

If you want a motivational environment, start with the person in the mirror. Be positive and passionate. Bring the room up every time you walk in. I tell our players all the time, "Champions pursue their passion—not a paycheck, and never a pension." If you're excellent at what you do, you'll be compensated. But if you want to be a champion, chase what you love. What wakes you up early and pulls you through the hard part of the day?

I've had the gift of doing this for nearly four decades, and I still feel like I'm heading out to recess. That's the goal. Love the work so much it feels like play, then do it with professional standards.

And remember how a real locker room is built: older players teach the younger players. That's the secret sauce. Seniors model the standard. Juniors echo it. Sophomores learn it. Freshmen catch it. The culture passes from heart to heart, rep to rep. That's how a kid learns what it really means to be a Falcon, a Badger, a Ram—whatever your colors. The values are lived out in the way veterans correct technique, share notes, pick up a teammate, and motivate daily with the core things we believe.

Lead with passion that people can feel. Keep the tone high, the standards clear, and the joy obvious. Do that, and motivation will stop being something you talk about and become the very air they breathe.

CHAPTER FOUR

CAPTURING THE MOMENT

THERE'S A PHRASE I've carried with me my whole life: "Capture the moment." And I'm not just talking about football. I'm talking about life. "Capture the moment" means living it fully. Living it fiercely and with urgency, intensity, and gratitude.

Capture the moment is a way of being. It's a mindset that starts the second your feet hit the floor in the morning. That means no snooze button, no alarm clock needed. If you need an alarm to drag yourself out of bed, you might need to find something different to wake up for. Because when you love what you do, when you know your purpose and pursue it with fire, you don't *wake up*—you launch into the day. You fly and hit the ground running every single day.

This isn't about hype—it's about mental, physical, emotional, and spiritual preparation. When you're truly present, you catch the beauty in a sunrise, the craft of a perfectly cooked meal, the precision of a linebacker bursting through the A gap, and in each of those moments lies an opportunity to make the block, hit the shot, and serve others with your gifts.

The truth is *you don't rise to the occasion—you fall to the level of your preparation.* When your number is called—and it will be called—you'd better be ready because there may be no warning. Whether or not you seize it depends entirely on the work you've already put in.

You prepare by studying the opponent's tendencies until you can read them like your own playbook. You drill it in walk-throughs, in jog-throughs, in full-speed reps under pressure. You chase competitive memory through relentless, exhausting repetition. You do the hard thing the right way, over and over again.

You might only get one shot. When opportunity and preparation collide, *that's* the moment. That's when you block the shot or score the touchdown. That's when you show the world what happens when *ready* meets *willing.*

Don't wait for your number to be called to get ready. *Live ready.*

THE MAN IN THE ARENA

If you want to *capture the moment,* you've got to love being the man in the arena. It's not enough to show up. It's not enough to play it safe or hang back in the stands where it's comfortable, where the lights aren't so hot, and the critics can't reach you. No, you've got to step into the arena. That's where the real work is.

President Theodore Roosevelt said it best in 1910, in his famous speech "Citizenship in a Republic." He didn't write it for the critics. He didn't write it for the crowd. He wrote it for the men and women willing to get their hands dirty, to sweat and bleed and fail and rise again—the ones who *dare greatly.*

In part, he said, "It is not the critic who counts.... The credit belongs to the man who is actually in the arena ... who errs, who comes short again and again ... but who does actually strive to do the deeds."

I'll tell you what: most people don't want it. Most people are specta-tors. They're happy in the bleachers, warm pretzel in one hand, pointing fingers with the other. They love to judge, to boo, to comment, but they'll never walk onto that field. When you walk onto that field, you're vulnerable. You're exposed. You're saying, "Here I am. Judge me by what I do."

Players do that. Players put themselves on the line. They know the risks—the fumbles, the missed shots—but they also know the thrill of victory. They know the celebration in the locker room that is earned through sweat and scars. That kind of joy is unforgettable, but you don't get that from the cheap seats.

When you capture the moment, you're honoring the stage. That stage might be a stadium, a classroom, a boardroom, or your own living room. Whatever it is, you show up with relentless effort and a full heart. You bring your best. You *love what you do,* and you *do what you love.*

That's what it means to be in the arena. So ask yourself today: are you willing to be the man or woman in the arena? Are you willing to be judged? Are you willing to *compete,* to *risk,* to *fail*?

I promise you this—the person who puts it all on the line, who plays with passion and pride and purpose—that person may fall, but they'll never be a cold and timid soul who knows neither victory nor defeat.

The locker room is not for sale, but if you've earned your spot in the arena, there's always a seat for you.

COMPETITIVE EXCELLENCE VERSUS CAPTURING THE MOMENT

There's one night I'll never forget. We were at Wisconsin, playing Ohio State under the lights in Madison. They were ranked number three in the country, and it was pouring rain. It was the kind of relentless downpour that soaks through your shoes and leaves your playbook soggy. The kind of weather that tests your preparation and your will to compete.

We lost our starting quarterback, Jim Sorgi, in the first quarter after he was choked at the bottom of a pile. His larynx was crushed so badly he couldn't speak—a first for me as a coach. The game had to go on, and it did, under sheets of torrential rain.

Our backup quarterback, Matt Schabert, was suddenly the conductor of this band of Badger brothers. The moment he'd always dreamed of— national TV, a packed Camp Randall, one of the biggest games of the year against Ohio State—was now his reality. The pregame storyline had been a showdown of All-Americans: Wisconsin's electric, sure-handed Lee Evans versus Ohio State's dynamic corner, Chris Gamble.

Tied 10–10 with five minutes left, we'd already thrown a couple of out routes to Evans to set things up, none completed. Our star still had zero catches late in the fourth. Then, in the biggest moment, we dialed up the jerk route. Evans gave Gamble the look, snapped his hips to sell the out, and exploded upfield. Schabert hit him in stride. Eighty yards later, the end zone erupted, and so did Camp Randall.

That right there was competitive excellence.

Urban Meyer defines competitive excellence as "making the play when your number is called," and he's right.[1] That touchdown wasn't luck. It was the result of reps on reps on reps. Walk-throughs, practice drills, film study, mental reps. Lee Evans had *earned* that moment long before the crowd ever roared.

But here's the key distinction: competitive excellence is what allows you to *make* the play. Capturing the moment is what makes the play unforgettable.

Competitive excellence is built in the dark: in practice fields, film rooms, and early mornings where no one's watching. It's mastering your craft so thoroughly that when the lights come on, you're not guessing or struggling to figure out what to do. You're just executing. But capturing the moment is something deeper. That's turning preparation

---

1. Urban Meyer with Wayne Coffey, *Above the Line: Lessons in Leadership and Life from a Championship Season* (Penguin Press, 2015).

*Lee Evans celebrating in the end zone with teammates on historic night
against Ohio State (Photo © Wisconsin Athletics—David Stluka)*

into a memory. It's putting a frame around the moment and stamping it into the story of your life.

This is what Lee Evans and Matt Schabert did, and this moment is firmly stamped in the story of their lives as this magical throw and catch has been ranked as one of the Top 100 Moments in Camp Randall football history.

Capturing the moment starts with a vision of something worth chasing. That dream fuels your purpose, and purpose sets a plan in motion. Passion drives that plan, and being *present*—fully locked in—gives you the opportunity to seize it when it comes. It's about knowing who you are, why you're here, and what you've been preparing for all along.

Both competitive excellence and capturing the moment demand relentless preparation. There's no shortcut there, but where competitive excellence is about execution, capturing the moment is about meaning. It's about that locker room celebration with your teammates, that memory you'll replay in your head when your playing days are

Matt Schabert rolling out to throw his magical pass to Lee Evans against Ohio State in 2003 (Photo © Wisconsin Athletics—David Stluka)

done. It's the story you'll tell your kids. The scar you'll point to with pride because scar tissue is championship tissue.

The beautiful thing is that this idea of capturing the moment isn't limited to sports. It's how you live. It's how you cook a meal. How you give a speech. How you raise a family. It becomes a way of being, a mindset that says, "When my number is called, I won't just show up. I'll leave a mark."

You need to strive for competitive excellence. You have to be ready, but when the time comes, don't just play the game—*capture the moment*. That's where the unforgettable stuff lives.

THE HURDLING HEBREW HAMMER

One of my all-time favorite examples of *capturing the moment* didn't come from a Heisman candidate or a first-round draft pick. It came from a fullback. A fullback who hadn't eaten all day. A fullback who wasn't supposed to carry the ball, let alone carry the team.

It was 2004, Wisconsin versus Penn State, a late Saturday afternoon kickoff. Matt Bernstein, a bruising 270-pounder from Scarsdale, New York, was our starting fullback. This particular Saturday happened to fall during Yom Kippur, the Jewish Day of Atonement, and that meant Matt couldn't eat until sundown. So our fullback was fasting, no food and no water, but he still suited up to play Big Ten football.

He broke his fast right there on the sideline during the first quarter. We had everything he loved waiting for him: cheeseburgers from Mickey's Dairy Bar, his favorite snacks, whatever it took to get his blood sugar back up and his body fueled.

And then came the moment.

We'd already lost our top four tailbacks. One by one, they went down. At halftime, Coach Barry Alvarez turned to me and said, "What are we going to do at tailback?"

I didn't hesitate. "We're putting Bernie back there."

He looked at me like I was crazy. "Bernstein? The fullback? You want to take the redshirt off someone else, maybe?"

"No, Coach," I said. "Bernie knows all the footwork. He's our best option. He'll be fine."

I meant it. Even though Matt had *never* taken a handoff in a game as a tailback, he had prepared like a champion. He showed up to every meeting. He studied every play. He knew the protections. He knew the details. And now, he was ready to show the world.

He went out and carried the ball twenty-six times for 120 yards. He *hurdled* defenders. He ran through tackles like they were made of tissue paper. The crowd fed off him. You could feel the electricity in Camp Randall. That night wasn't just another win. It was *history*.

Matt Bernstein with those "competitive eyes"
running through Penn State in 2004
(Photo © Wisconsin Athletics—David Stluka)

That performance has since been ranked as one of the top twenty-five moments in Wisconsin football history.

That night, he earned the nickname the *Hurdling Hebrew Hammer.*

Matt captured his moment and went down in history. Now, of course, he didn't dream of it. Not really. Fullbacks don't fantasize about starting at tailback. That's not in the script, but when the opportunity showed up, he didn't blink or hesitate. He was prepared, fully present, and ready.

You can't buy moments like that. You can only *earn* them with every rep. Preparation met opportunity, and Matt Bernstein seized it with both hands—and twenty-six carries. He was throwing hammers and hurdling defenders on all of those memorable runs. That's what capturing the moment looks like.

PREPARATION AND THE SIDELINE PROMISE

Every now and then, a moment comes along that reminds you exactly why you coach. It was 2022, and we were locked in a rivalry game against Toledo—the Battle of I-75. A cold night, third and 10, twenty-one seconds on the clock, and we were trailing 35 to 34. There was just one timeout left. On the sideline, the team was tense, locked in, waiting on the next call.

That's when *Taron "TK" Keith,* our tailback, came to life. He didn't wait for a play to be called. He didn't need permission. He walked straight up to our quarterback, Matt McDonald, and said, "Throw me the ball. I'm going to score." Not "I might," not "let's try this." Just pure conviction.

He explained to the quarterback, "I'm going to invite this defender to cover me. Then I'm going to juke him, run up the sideline, and take it to the house."

I tried to pull him back. "TK," I said, "Just do your job. We'll get into field goal range and win it the smart way. No hero ball."

He shook his head. "No, Coach. I'm scoring."

I've seen confidence in a lot of forms over the years, but this wasn't ego talking. I could tell TK meant it completely.

The ball was snapped. TK drifted to the right flat, just like he said he would, and sat there, baiting the nickel safety to press up. As soon as the defender bit, TK exploded off his break, cut back inside, and caught a clean ball in stride.

From there, it was poetry in motion. He weaved through six or seven defenders like they were stuck in mud. The crowd rose in waves as he crossed the goal line, sealing one of the most improbable finishes I've ever witnessed in thirty-nine years of coaching.

That wasn't a fluke. That was a preparation *meeting opportunity*—the very definition of capturing the moment.

We talk about it all the time in the locker room. You don't rise to the occasion—you fall to your level of training. TK had trained for that moment, whether he knew it or not. He was ready because he had done

Taron Keith scoring winning touchdown with eight seconds left in the Battle of I-75
(Photo © Bowling Green State University Athletics—Scott Grau)

the work. The reps, the meetings, the film, and the fundamentals had all prepared him to trust himself when it mattered most.

He didn't wait for someone to believe in him. He *believed in himself* first, and that belief turned into action, which turned into one of the greatest endings in Bowling Green football history.

You want to talk about capturing the moment? That was it. That was TK standing on his own Broadway stage, lights bright, pressure high, and delivering the performance of a lifetime. That touchdown became a memory burned into every player, coach, and fan in the stadium that night.

Sometimes, capturing the moment means listening to your gut when no one else sees it. It means being bold enough to call your own shot and being prepared enough to *hit* it. That's what leadership looks like. That's what preparation looks like.

YOU CAN'T CAPTURE THE SHOT IF YOU'RE ASLEEP

Capturing the moment isn't just a sports cliché. It's how you approach every single day of your life. Think of it like photography. You can't capture the perfect shot if you're distracted or asleep. You can't get the photo that tells the story, the one that lasts forever, if you're not paying attention.

The same is true in football, in business, in life. If your focus is scattered, if your heart's not in it, if you're pressing snooze instead of chasing purpose, you'll miss it. The opportunity comes, and it passes you by.

That's why I always say, "Passion is the oxygen of the soul." That's how I've lived my entire coaching life. I've never hit snooze because I've always had something I was excited to wake up to. If you're waking up dragging your feet, then something's wrong. There's nothing wrong with the clock, but with the life you're building around it. You don't need a louder alarm. You need a louder *explanation*.

Once you find that reason, it makes all the difference. However, if your life is full of distractions, if you're letting noise drown out your purpose, you'll never be fully focused. And without focus, you'll never capture anything that matters.

When you live with intention, when you're locked in on a dream, when you've built a plan and you execute it with discipline and fire, that's when you get the shot. That's when you're in the right place, with the right mindset, at the right time.

Preparation is the key to everything. Whether you're chasing a championship, building a business, or just trying to live a meaningful life: be prepared. But preparation alone isn't enough. It has to be fueled by *passion*. If you don't love what you do, you won't prepare the right way. You won't put in the extra reps. You won't study film late at night. You won't sweat the details or stay hungry when the road gets hard. Without passion, preparation becomes a checklist instead of a lifestyle.

That's why I tell my players, my coaches, my kids—actually, anybody who'll listen—you've got to *love what you do and do what you love*. When you're passionate, you wake up with a purpose. You wake up *running*.

At every stop along my coaching journey, we've had some version of this philosophy:

At Colorado State, we always said, "Wake up ramming." With the Falcons, we said, "Wake up flying." No matter the team, no matter the year, the message was always the same: Wake up with urgency. Wake up with purpose. Wake up prepared to capture the moment.

If you don't wake up with intention, you'll sleepwalk through your opportunities. And if you live your life hitting snooze, sooner or later, your moment will pass you by. This applies to sports, but it's just as true in business and in life. Greatness doesn't separate itself by domain. It separates itself by preparation and effort and waking up each day ready to *attack* it.

So whether you're heading into a game, a boardroom, or a kitchen table with your family, ask yourself, "Did I prepare? Did I bring the passion? Am I ready to win the day?" That's what it means to live a life that captures the moment.

PREPARING FOR DEFINING MOMENTS

So how do leaders prepare themselves and their teams to capture their defining moment? It all starts with passion. That's the fuel. You must believe *deeply* in what you're doing. That means *showing up with fire*. You need a reason to get up in the morning, a dream that propels you out of bed.

Once you have the dream, you build a blueprint. Then you activate that blueprint and go to work on it every day, relentlessly, until that dream becomes a reality. That's how you prepare.

But passion and planning aren't enough without a mindset to match. Great leaders don't think any job is beneath them. They bring a no-job-is-too-small mentality to everything they do. They set the tone, and they model what it looks like to attack the day with purpose. Just as important, they surround themselves with like-minded people who believe in the mission and prepare with the same intensity.

Whether you're leading a team, launching a company, raising a family, or chasing a goal of your own, it all comes down to preparation. And the only way preparation becomes powerful is when it's fueled by passion. So wake up with purpose. Build your plan. Activate it. And get after it every single day so you're ready when it counts. The moment *will* come, and when it does, you'll be the one who's ready to own it.

THE SHOT NO ONE ELSE GOT

Some moments in life are just too perfect to script and too powerful to miss. I'll never forget the 1999 Rose Bowl. It was one of the most iconic games of my coaching career, a back-and-forth battle that came down to the final play. On that last snap, Wendell Bryant broke through the line and sacked the quarterback. The crowd erupted. The game was over.

President Reagan, Salli White, and President Mikhail Gorbachev
celebrating the crumbling of the Berlin Wall (Photo © Salli White)

What made it truly unforgettable is that my wife captured it all on camera. Now, you've got to understand, my wife isn't just someone with a camera. She's a professional photographer. Earlier in her career, she was one of Ronald Reagan's official photographers. But that night, she was standing on the sidelines with her lens, soaking in the energy like everyone else.

When the game ended and the photos started circulating, we realized that no one else got the shot. Not the AP. Not UPI. Not the dozens of professional media outlets lined up with their gear. Only my wife had the frame of Wendell bursting through the blocker, slamming the quarterback to the turf, and sealing the win.

I asked her, "How were you the only one to catch it?"

She just smiled and said, "I don't know. I had a feeling."

That's the essence of capturing the moment. It's not luck. It's being present, focused, and tuned in to the energy in the air. She trusted her instinct and kept the lens trained on the quarterback, and when her moment came, she was ready. That photograph became a piece of

Wendell Bryant making a game-ending sack at the 1999 Rose Bowl
(Photo © Salli White)

Wisconsin football history. It froze in time what every player, coach, and fan felt in their bones.

I have another shot I took myself years later while recruiting in New York City. I was walking across the Manhattan Bridge early one morning when I looked up and saw the Empire State Building perfectly framed through the steel supports. It was just sitting there, waiting to be noticed. That's what these moments are like. They don't announce themselves. They don't wait around. You either see them, or you don't.

This reminds me of a quote from my sister Geralyn, Executive Producer of multiple Oscar-winning documentaries, "Visionaries don't ask people to enlist, they just join the mission because it captures their soul." These moments just happen, and you must always be ready to capture it.

In football, in life, in leadership, the people who make history aren't always the flashiest or even the best prepared on paper. They're the ones who never take their eyes off the moment.

Capturing the Moment in New York City (Photo © Brian White)

CHAPTER FIVE

PLAY HARD, BE A GREAT TEAMMATE

FOOTBALL IS THE definition of a team sport, and I don't say that lightly. I've coached a lot of games over a lot of years, and I can tell you without a doubt that no one wins alone out there. Not in this game.

It takes eleven players doing their job with precision and passion every single play. That's the deal. That's the standard. If even one guy blows his assignment, the whole thing can fall apart. A missed block turns into a sack. A lazy route becomes an interception. A busted coverage gives up six points. That's football. It's not about one person's stats; it's about collective execution.

Every play is a trust exercise. When that ball is snapped, I have to believe every guy on the field is going to handle his responsibility like it's the most important job in the world because at that moment, it is.

Even the greatest quarterback in the world can't win games without protection from his O-line, without receivers who run crisp routes, without running backs who know their assignments. The same goes for defense, where it's gap integrity, pursuit angles, and communication. Everybody's role matters. There's no hiding. That's why we say football doesn't just build character—it reveals it.

WHAT MAKES A GREAT TEAM MEMBER?

So what makes someone a great teammate? It starts with *accountability*—doing your job even when no one's watching. That means showing up early, staying late, helping the guy next to you because you know your success is tied to the success of the man or woman beside you.

Great team members put the team first. They don't care who gets the credit as long as the job gets done. They encourage and challenge their teammates to be better, and they're consistent. That's the thing most people miss. Talent can come and go, but character endures.

Being a great teammate isn't flashy. A great teammate is dependable, disciplined, and driven. They wake up every day and choose to bring their best, not for the spotlight, but for the brotherhood. And in football, that's everything.

What makes someone a great team member? It starts with being *selfless*. That's the foundation. A great teammate understands they're part of something bigger than themselves. When you're on a team— whether it's football, business, or life—you must be willing to sacrifice individual glory for the good of the group. That doesn't mean you shrink your impact. It means you pour everything you have into the role you've been given and take pride in the collective result. Winning is a *we* thing, not a *me* thing.

The second trait is *loyalty*. And I'm not just talking about loyalty when things are going well. I'm talking about locker room loyalty, the kind that shows up when the heat's on and there's chatter in the background. Football teams are big. We've got 110 guys in the building, and with that many personalities, conflict and pressure are inevitable. So loyalty to your teammates, to the coaching staff, and to the mission of the team has to be nonnegotiable. Trust is fragile, and one disloyal act can tear down a culture that took years to build.

Next up is *work ethic*. Look, people admire talent, but they *respect* work habits. Everybody loves the highlight reel, but what really makes the difference overall is the guy who punches in and punches out, day after day, without needing a camera on him. Great teammates bring consistency. They show up early, stay late, hold themselves accountable, and raise the standard for everybody else.

Finally, great teammates *celebrate with others*. I tell my guys all the time, "You're not a one-man band." When you make a great play, go find your brothers. Celebrate with the linemen who opened the hole. Acknowledge the quarterback who delivered the pass. That's how you build something special—by spreading the glory and making the team feel like family.

Some of the best moments in football don't show up on the stat sheet, like when a running back scores a touchdown and runs straight to hug the offensive lineman who paved the way. That's what this game is about. That's what *life* is about.

Be selfless. Be loyal. Outwork everybody. And celebrate your teammates. That's the kind of player who makes a locker room worth fighting for.

"Play as hard as you can, as fast as you can,
for as long as you can—
and be a great teammate."

This has been my mantra for years. It's something I've shared with every player I've coached, and it's a philosophy that reaches far beyond the football field. It's a way of life.

Play as hard as you can. That means putting in relentless, unyielding, full-throttle effort. Don't coast. Don't jog. Don't go halfway. Bring everything you've got, every single time. Whether it's practice or game day, show up with urgency and intensity.

Play as fast as you can. Football is a game of speed—not just physical speed, but mental quickness, decisiveness, and the ability to react and respond in real time. Fast players make plays. Fast minds make adjustments. If you can go fast *and* do your job right, you become a difference-maker.

Play for as long as you can. This is about grit and stamina. How long can you maintain your focus, energy, and commitment? Go until you're empty, and when you hit that wall, raise your hand, come out, and let the next man go to work. This is a team, and when one player steps out, another steps up.

And through it all, *be a great teammate.* That's the glue that holds it together. A great teammate is selfless. A great teammate is accountable. A great teammate doesn't just play *with* others—they play *for* others. They celebrate the wins together and shoulder the losses together. They uplift and protect. They sacrifice.

If you live this mindset—not just in football, but in life—you'll find yourself surrounded by people who trust you, believe in you, and are willing to go to battle with you. That's what championship culture is made of.

THE POWER OF CELEBRATION

Celebrating with your teammates is the heartbeat of football. This is something that happens in the locker room all the time. It's not about pounding your chest and saying, "Look at me." It's about wrapping your arms around the people who battled beside you and saying, "We did it." That's where the real brotherhood is built.

The moments I cherish most in this game aren't always the touchdowns or the final scores. They're the pictures we hang up in the running backs' room, pictures that show guys celebrating together. Those are the snapshots of joy, unity, and brotherhood. That's what players remember years later. They don't recall the scoreboard, but who stood next to them in the trenches and who celebrated with them when the job was done.

I'll never forget my first taste of that magic. Back when I was just getting started coaching at Fordham with Larry Glueck, we pulled off a stunning upset in the Division III playoffs against Hofstra. It was late November, bone-chilling cold—minus twenty with the wind chill. No one gave us a chance. The year before, Hofstra beat us 41–6.

This time, we flipped the script. We out-physicaled them, outplayed them, and walked off with a 41–8 win. That locker room afterward was pure joy. Guys were laughing, hugging, tears in their eyes. It was beautiful.

Then there was the 1999 Rose Bowl. We were massive underdogs going into that game against UCLA. The game was in their backyard, but it felt like Madison South with seventy thousand Badger fans packing the Rose Bowl. When that clock hit zero and we'd secured the win, that locker room erupted. That celebration was about a team proving something to the world and to themselves. It was about legacy.

The Florida-Georgia rivalry is one of college football's greatest. Always the last Saturday in October, it is like playing a bowl game in the middle of the season. As the bus takes you to the stadium, you know this is special as you can feel the energy of the fans when you step off the bus. It's electric. A stadium divided in half by the Gators' blue and orange and Georgia's black and red. It is known as the World's Largest Cocktail Party. On this day in 2014, the Florida Gators rushed for an amazing 418 yards in a 38–20 victory. Tailbacks Matt Jones and Kelvin Taylor had career and almost identical days. Matt had 192 yards on twenty-five carries, and Kelvin roughed up the Bulldogs for 197 yards on another twenty-five carries. A punishing performance for sure, and a magical locker room celebration followed. Head Coach Will Muschamp, a player's coach and a coach's coach, enjoyed every second of the overflowing joy, reveling in a team that really played in his blue-collar reflection. A locker room I will never forget.

While at Boston College, the 2017 "Red Bandanna" win over Florida State and the 2018 "Red Bandanna" win over Miami were special locker-room celebrations. The Red Bandanna Game honors 9/11 hero and former BC lacrosse player Welles Crowther, who selflessly gave his life to save others on that tragic day. Celebrating with his parents in the locker room—and hearing how much Welles loved being part of a team, loved being a BC man, and lived the Boston College mantra, "men and women for others"—was profoundly humbling. Their words still give me chills.

More recently, I've seen that same joy right here at Bowling Green. Three times now, we've beaten Toledo in the Battle of I-75—our biggest

Victory celebration at Toledo in 2022
(Photo © Bowling Green State University Athletics—Mallory Hiser)

rivalry. The game three years ago came down to the wire. Taron Keith, one of the gutsiest players I've ever coached, made a last-second catch and run that defied explanation. He weaved through half their defense and scored. The stadium exploded, but it was the locker room after that win that was unforgettable—players singing, coaches grinning ear to ear, every face lit up with joy. It's a feeling that stays with you.

October 11, 2025, is a Saturday I'll never forget—the rivalry game against Toledo, the Battle of I-75. Toledo dominated the first half and led 21–0 with just over a minute left before halftime. Then came a historic surge: 28 unanswered points and a dramatic 28–23 victory. It was truly a game for the ages—arguably the greatest comeback in school history—and the locker room afterward was unforgettable!

And I'll never forget the Border War win at Colorado State. We were up against Wyoming, playing for the Bronze Boot. We weren't favored, but we came out on top, 34–24. Trey McBride, one of the best tight ends in the league now, had a huge game. The second the final

Bowling Green locker room celebrating historic comeback win against rival Toledo on October 11, 2025 (Photo © Bowling Green State University Athletics—Kate Laney)

whistle blew, our team sprinted across the field to grab that boot. I've got a photo of it—players running with arms wide, eyes lit up like kids on Christmas morning. That image is etched in my mind. That's what this game is all about.

You see, football isn't just about plays—it's about people. And when you pour everything you've got into something bigger than yourself, and you *win together,* that deserves celebration. That's where the bonds are forged. That's where the memories are made, and that's why the locker room is not for sale.

THE PRIDE OF THE LOCKER ROOM

When people talk about leadership in football, they usually picture the quarterback or the head coach. But if you want to understand the *soul* of a team, it starts in a place most people overlook: the locker room. In every great locker room, there's one person behind the scenes who quietly sets the tone.

Let me tell you something most fans don't know: the culture of every locker room in America is built by the equipment manager. At every stop in my coaching journey, I've seen firsthand how these silent leaders shape the pride and identity of a team. One of the best examples I can give you is my best friend, Paul "Pooch" Pucciarelli, who served as the equipment manager at UNLV for more than thirty years. That's thirty years of excellence. Thirty years of showing up, doing the work, and taking pride in the little things. That's leadership.

Pooch didn't just pass out gear—he built a culture. He taught players the unspoken lessons of the locker room: be meticulous, be organized, follow instructions, and above all, *take pride in your space.* A locker room isn't just where you hang your pads—it's where you learn discipline, accountability, and respect. It's where the older players teach the younger ones how to prepare like pros and how to leave the space better than they found it.

Game day is when the magic really hits you. You walk into that locker room, and it feels like Christmas morning. The helmets are lined up and gleaming. The jerseys are pressed and folded just right. Every detail is flawless. It's a signal to the players that *this matters*. That they're part of something special. That someone took the time to create a space worthy of the stage they're about to step onto.

Guys like Pooch don't ask for recognition, but they're the heartbeat of every great program. They make it possible for the players to walk into the arena with their heads high, feeling like warriors dressed for battle. They make sure the stage is set both physically *and* emotionally. And when that locker room is pristine and humming with energy, every player in that room knows: *It's time.*

If you want to talk about unsung heroes, start with the people who build the culture when no one's looking. The ones who believe that excellence in the small things creates the foundation for greatness in the big ones. That's the power of the locker room.

UNLV pregame locker room filled with precision and pride
(Photo © UNLV Photo Services)

Not all leaders wear captain patches. Not all heroes score touchdowns. Some of the most important people in any locker room are the ones you rarely hear about. They're not standing in front of the camera. They're not spiking the ball in the end zone. But every day, without needing to be asked, they do the things that matter. They do the little things *right*.

These silent leaders don't ask for recognition. They don't chase attention. What they do is protect the standard. They're the ones who walk the locker room after practice, picking up tape and trash left behind. They don't do it because someone told them to, but because they care too much to let the space be disrespected. They believe the locker room is sacred, and they're not about to let it slide on their watch.

You'll usually find them on the scout team. They might not see the field on Saturdays, but they're preparing the team every single day to be their best. They set the tone and model accountability. And they don't need applause to know their value. I've never forgotten guys like that.

When I was in college, I played with a guy named Bernie Guekgezian. He was a defensive lineman—not a starter or a superstar—but Bernie was the heart and soul of our locker room. He lived with integrity and treated everyone around him with respect. Today, he continues to be a "great teammate," and he's one of the most respected lawyers in Boston. That doesn't surprise me one bit.

Then there was Gerry Leone. He didn't play a ton either, but no one outworked him. Not one guy. His effort was relentless. His discipline was unwavering, and his teammates saw it. They felt it. Gerry didn't need a title to be a leader. He lived it every day. He went on to become the district attorney of Massachusetts, serving with the same integrity he brought to the field.

These are the guys I think about when people ask me what builds a great team. It's not just the superstars. It's the ones in the shadows, the ones who do the work without fanfare, who pass down values from one class to the next. They hold the locker room together, and every team—*every single team*—has them. If you look closely, you'll see them. And if you're lucky, you'll be one of them.

They prove that real leadership isn't loud; it's *lived*. In the locker room, that's what makes all the difference.

CHAPTER SIX

THE CHAMPION'S PROFILE

EVERY SEASON, BEFORE a whistle blows or a scoreboard lights up, I hand our players a simple sheet of paper. It's not a playbook or a depth chart. Those come later. No, the first thing I hand them is something I call the Champion's Profile, which is a way of life boiled down to one page. If you want a championship team, build championship people. This is the blueprint.

Being a champion starts with passion. When you wake up in the morning and your feet hit the floor, you're already moving. Champions do what they love and love what they do. They are doers who build success on boring, relentless consistency.

I learned to be a "doer" from my mother. She's now eighty-six years old and still a force of nature. If you meet her for two seconds, you'll feel it. She used to tell me, "If you want something done, give it to the busiest person." In other words, give it to a "doer" because if it's on their plate, it is going to get finished.

That's the first line of the Champion's Profile: *be a doer*. Wake up running. Wake up ramming. Wake up ready. Attack the day.

But passion needs a target. Champions dream with confetti falling. They see the stage, the lights, the scoreboard reading the right way, and then they build a plan to make that dream inevitable. Dream big, then go to work. Put a game plan on paper, execute it on purpose, and hold yourself to the standard relentlessly.

Conviction is the engine. Confidence is the fuel. Energy is the spark that ignites it. You earn conviction through preparation so thoroughly that you've got the answers to the test before the test. Champions are maniacal about preparation. They are fanatical about it. They refuse to be denied or to be insignificant.

The next line of the Champion's Profile says, "Play as hard as you can, as fast as you can, for as long as you can. And be a great teammate." Be selfless in the huddle and ruthless in the rep. Champions create bonds that hold under pressure. They believe first in the mission, then in each other, and always in themselves. They believe in their coaches. They believe in the work. Belief is the bridge you sprint across to reach the goal.

Resilience is nonnegotiable. Every season will throw a few sucker punches, but champions always get up and go on to the next play. They have uncommon poise, which enables them to keep moving without stopping or slowing down. You will make mistakes; everyone does. The question is how quickly you reset your eyes, your breathing, your focus, and get back into the game. Champions return to "drive" faster than anyone else, and they do it together.

Champions love the competitive arena. If you give them a stage, they'll give you a show. They don't merely chase attention. They crave victory, and the bigger the moment, the clearer they get on what needs to be done. They capture the moment for all to see and then hand the game ball to the team. That's the paradox of the great ones: they compete selfishly—"Every rep is mine!"—but they give selflessly—"Every win is ours."

Loyalty matters. We're not a collection of independent contractors. We're a team. Champions protect the locker room and hold each other accountable without making it personal. They finish things without excuses—from whistle to whistle and season to season. And when it's done, they celebrate together because they built it together.

Champions have passion with a plan, conviction earned by preparation, confidence rooted in work, and energy you can feel across the field. So be a doer. Dream with confetti. Play hard, fast, and long. Reset with poise. I love the arena. Stay loyal. Finish. Then—and only then—do you get to throw your arms around your brothers and let the confetti actually fall.

BOWLING GREEN FALCONS – CHAMPION'S PROFILE

- **BG Champions wake up flying.** No alarm clocks needed. Others set multiple alarms and hit multiple snooze buttons.
- **BG Champions do.** Others don't. Be a doer, not a don'ter.
- **BG Champions play as hard as they can, as fast as they can, for as long as they can—and they're great teammates.**
- **BG Champions attack every day head-on.** They love direct, face-to-face contact—all-out assault, no shortcuts needed. Others look for the easy way, shortcuts, and corner-cutting.
- **BG Champions live "Green Means Go."** They are accelerators—full-throttle, pedal-to-the-metal, tough guys who love to compete. Others live in the yellow world of caution, tiptoeing through the day—toe-tappers versus

jump-in-the-water guys.

- **BG Champions dream big dreams—dreams with confetti falling—and then attack those dreams.** They activate their dreams with a game plan and then execute the plan to perfection. Others have no vision to dream.

- **BG Champions exude passion.** They have a bounce in their step that says they love what they do and do what they love. Passion is the relentless pursuit of perfection— never the pursuit of a paycheck. Champions pursue their passion, never their pension.

- **BG Champions create blood—bleed orange and brown.** They love the team. Others are too cautious to ever bleed.

- **BG Champions believe.** They believe in themselves, their teammates, and their coaches. They have conviction. Others live in the cloudy world of doubt, maybes, and indecision.

- **BG Champions have a plan to win, believe in the plan to win, follow the plan to win—and win.** Others have no plan; they're schemers.

- **BG Champions prepare to win.** They have the answers to the test before the test through preparation. Others buy Cliff Notes.

- **BG Champions play with relentless, fanatical, never-to-be-denied effort—point A to point B as fast as you can.** Others play hard only when it's convenient and comfortable.

- **BG Champions play with uncommon poise.** When something bad happens, they play the next play with incredible focus, tenacity, and concentration—concentrated reps. Others fold like a cheap suit when it gets hard—leaders of the "Bitch Brigade."

- **BG Champions have Falcon Eyes—"Live Eyes," competitive eyes, winning eyes—Tiger/Jordan/LeBron eyes.** Others have dull, listless, tired eyes.
- **BG Champions love the competitive arena.** They love being "the man in the arena" for all to see and watch. The bigger the stage, the brighter the lights, the better they play. Others like watching and being spectators.
- **BG Champions thrive in the most competitive moments.** They make the play when their number is called. This is our gold standard called "Competitive Excellence." Others hope someone else gets their number called.
- **BG Champions give selflessly—the team, the team, the team.** Others want selfishly.
- **BG Champions are BG Warriors who are loyal and live the values of a BG Falcon.** Others are independent contractors loyal to nothing.
- **BG Champions know how to finish—fourth quarter.** Others ask for extensions.
- **BG Champions celebrate together—chest bumps, high fives, fist bumps.** Others endorse themselves: "Look at me."
- **BG Champions find a way to win—and sing the fight song loud and proud:** "Ay Ziggy Zoomba, Zoomba, Zoomba! Ay Ziggy Zoomba, Zoomba Ze!"

PASSION IS CAUGHT, NOT TAUGHT

Passion isn't a lecture. It's not something you memorize—it's something you feel. It's kinetic, the ultimate force multiplier, and like compound interest, it grows on itself: one spark becomes a flame, one flame becomes a fire, and soon the whole locker room is warm. While I was coaching at Boston College, team chaplain Father Jack Butler was that kind of force multiplier. He was a force of nature you caught every time you heard his distinctive voice, met his steady eyes, and took in his "catchable" wisdom and guidance. A true servant leader, Father Jack will become the twenty-sixth president of Boston College in July 2026. I'm confident he'll keep throwing "passion to the people" for all to catch and pass on.

You'll forget half of what people tell you, but you'll never forget how they make you feel. That's why great teachers, coaches, and teammates change a room the second they walk in—you can feel their love for the work. It's authentic, not manufactured, and because it's real, it spreads. Passion isn't pushed from a podium. It's transmitted heart to heart through example, energy, and effort. Steve Addazio and Frank Leonard—best friends, loyal as the day is long—brought that passion in daily doses. You could feel it, pulsing with purpose. Just ask any Boston College athlete.

Passion is purpose-driven. It's the most powerful renewable energy source on earth, and it lives in the human spirit, hungry for the human touch to pass it on. Champions don't chase pensions or paychecks. They pursue passion. They dream big, and then they lace those dreams to old-fashioned hard work. Passion is the oxygen of the soul. Keep breathing it, and your "why" stops being a question and starts being a compass.

That's why we build teams that feel it first and explain it second. When passion is alive, conviction and confidence follow.

CONVICTION, CONFIDENCE, AND THE WAR ON SELF-DOUBT

Conviction means having faith in your path. It's a belief that is clear, lived-in, and tested. Believe in yourself. Believe in your teammates. Believe in your coaches.

But conviction doesn't appear out of thin air. It has to rest on something solid. You need core beliefs you can name and defend, things like gratitude, grit, selflessness, and loyalty. Whatever your core values are, conviction is the decision to attack your day in alignment with them, on purpose, without apology.

Confidence is different. Confidence is the by-product of relentless preparation. It's the work that drives more work, the focus that compounds into mastery. Confidence is that moment when obsessive preparation meets competitive excellence, and you make the play because you are ready—because you've *been* ready. When your number is called, you don't flinch or hesitate. You autograph the moment boldly.

That road that leads to real confidence is often lonely and dark, with detours that make you question the map. You'll be frustrated, confused, tempted to turn around. Keep going. Confidence is a journey that pays you back for a lifetime because you chose the hard reps when nobody was watching.

The thing that tries to steal your confidence is self-doubt. In fact, self-doubt is the number one challenge for young athletes stepping into college sports. Yesterday's top dog became today's freshman. Suddenly, they're on a new campus with a new playbook. There's no familiar bed down the hall. So the questions rush in: *Am I good enough? Do I belong here? Is this really for me?*

This is where coaching matters most. Great coaches anticipate self-doubt and deal with it before it rears its head. As Barry Alvarez would remind us, "Think like a shortstop." In other words, expect the ball, know the situation, and be ready before the play starts. With young players, that means we address self-doubt before it blooms. We talk about the transition and normalize the struggle. We connect belief to behaviors they control.

Here's how we do it:

- **Name the standard, then teach the process.** Confidence lives in the plan, through film habits, lift habits, practice habits, nutrition, and sleep. When athletes see the link between inputs and outcomes, belief turns from hope into evidence.
- **Anchor to core values.** We don't just post words on a wall. We practice them. Gratitude shows up in how we receive coaching. Grit shows up on rep ten when the legs are burning. Selflessness shows up in how we celebrate a teammate's snap count, not just our own.
- **Celebrate preparation, not just performance.** If we only praise the scoreboard, we teach kids to chase approval. When we praise the work, we teach them to build confidence where it's strongest—and in their control.
- **Reset fast.** Mistakes happen. Champions play the next play with poise. Breathe, refocus, then execute. Confidence grows every time you prove to yourself you can recover.

Conviction and confidence are cousins. Conviction tells you *who you are*, then confidence proves *what you can do*. Together, they silence self-doubt. You don't "talk" your way into belief—you work your way into it. And when your name gets called, you won't need a speech because you'll have your preparation and your values.

A CHAMPION'S CONFIDENCE CREED

Confidence, very simply, is belief. It is believing you are
good. It is knowing you are good without any unnecessary
self-promotion. It is believing in yourself, believing in
your teammates, and believing in your coaches.

Confidence is the by-product of demanding, exacting,
precise, thorough preparation. Very simply, it is work.
Work that drives; work that engages. Work that elevates
people to stratospheric levels of self-satisfied, completely
fulfilled achievement. You will work hard as a Falcon, and
that is the way it's supposed to be when you earn goals
worth working for. Confidence is that one moment in
time when unbelievably focused preparation produces
spectacular results through competitive excellence. It is
making the play when your number is called because you
are "the man in the arena"—competing for all to see and
judge. You embrace the moment because you have relentlessly prepared for the moment and can't wait to "own the
moment" and put your signature on the moment for all to
know, and remember: bold, clear, legible signature—autograph your work

Confidence is the road less traveled. It can be a
lonely road. It can be a dark road. It can be an isolated
road. It can be a road that has multiple detours but
it is a road that will take you on a journey, not to a
destination. This road will frustrate, confuse, inhibit,
stagger, tempt and hold back but it will also inspire,
motivate, and lead to a lifetime of staggering successes.

The championship road less traveled is under constant construction.

Confidence is what occurs when good, honest, hard work is rewarded with the achievement you designed. Design the ring through the sweat equity you all pour into being a champion and always grinding for greatness.

Confidence is the right that you deserve if and only if you have earned it! Keep grinding together and enjoy the competitive challenge that will be presented by this great sport.

WHEN DOUBT KNOCKS, RUN THROUGH IT

Every great career experiences moments that feel like the end. I've watched this happen up close many, many times. I can think of countless champions who had long camp days or a depth chart that looked like a mountain. So what do you do when doubt shows up?

I remember a freshman back named Ron Dayne who came into camp a little heavy and a lot human. Due to his size, he was recruited by many as a fullback, but he started the year third or fourth on the tailback line. He began to wonder if everyone else had been right.

"Coach, maybe I'm a fullback," he said.

My message was simple and on repeat: "Keep working. Keep stacking days. It will click."

We went into that third game, and the first half on the ground was a disaster. We got negative rushing yards and had zero rhythm.

At halftime, I said, "OK, let's see what the kid can do."

In the second half, we got the football in his hands, he dominated the fourth quarter, and we won the game. He earned the start, ran for more than two thousand yards as a freshman, and the rest became trophy-case history. But don't romanticize it. That night wasn't magic. It was months of work meeting one open door.

Years later, another freshman back named A. J. Dillon (who would become an all-American) sat in my office during camp and said the line I hear from almost every first-year: "Coach, I don't know if I'm improving. I don't know if I'm good enough."

My answer didn't change: "Stay with the process. Your legs will catch up to your mind."

Week six arrived on the road against a superstar quarterback and a ranked opponent, and the kid exploded for 275 yards. Before kickoff, I couldn't promise that. I could only promise that our belief would be stronger than his doubt, and our standard would not move.

Positive coaching is powerful coaching. You can be demanding without being demeaning. In fact, that's the only way to develop freshmen. Hold the bar high, correct with clarity, and never take a player's dignity to make a point. I want my guys to tell you I was relentless about details and ruthless about effort—and that I never belittled them. Standards rise when people feel respected.

The transition to college is harder than most people realize. You go from top dog to starting over, all while dealing with homesickness. I tell recruits and parents the same honest truth in every living room: "You will feel it. If you don't build real relationships with your coaches and teammates, if you're not honest with yourself, with your family, and with us, you'll struggle more than you need to."

There are no shortcuts through that tunnel. You talk and ask for help. You show up to the weight room and the film room on the days you least want to. You stay coachable. You let your preparation build evidence, and you let that evidence build confidence. Then one day, when the moment finally arrives, you won't hesitate. You'll put your foot in the ground, trust your training, and show the world (and yourself) what you're capable of.

Doubt can visit. It just doesn't get the ball.

THE WALK-ON WHO MOVED A LOCKER ROOM

Andy Strader came to Boston College as a walk-on out of a powerhouse program in Southern California. On paper, he was "undersized." He lacked the measurables scouts brag about, but from day one, he had two things that don't fit neatly in a spreadsheet: an engine and a standard. He worked hard, and he competed hard. He did whatever was asked of him. For the scout team, he was a problem every Tuesday. For special teams, he found a way to help, even returning a couple of kicks when his number was called.

He battled the same self-doubt every freshman experiences. *Am I good enough? Do I belong at this level?* He answered those questions the only way that matters: with habits. That meant showing up early, owning the lift, crushing the rep, and learning the game plan like he was starting on Saturday. He did this daily, relentlessly.

By the time he was a senior, something beautiful had happened. The depth chart still didn't announce his name in lights, but the locker room did. Teammates mirrored his effort. Coaches trusted his voice. The program felt his fingerprint, and at season's end, he received Boston College's Scanlan Award—the highest honor our athletes can earn—recognizing his leadership, scholastic excellence, and athletic excellence.

Bear in mind that he never "won" a game by himself. He won something bigger because he moved a whole team to greatness.

That's the power of belief and the impact it can make in a healthy locker room. Respect isn't handed to you with a starting job. It's earned behind the scenes when nobody's cheering. Andy proved that impact isn't limited to snaps played or stats posted. Impact is a culture you carry with you and leak onto everyone around you.

For every Heisman story, there's an Andy Strader story. A walk-on who outlasted doubt and outled his résumé. That's why we coach the way we do—demanding without demeaning—because the overlooked kid might be the one who lifts the whole locker room. When that happens, it can change what a team believes about itself.

Mom Camille Strader, Brian White, Andy Strader, and Dad Tim Strader
(Photo © Brian White)

CHAPTER SEVEN

FALCON EYES

WHEN I STUDY great competitors, I start with the eyes. Not the forty time or the vertical. The eyes. They tell you everything. Eyes reveal confidence, hunger, poise, the truth about whether a player wants the ball when it matters. Early in my career, I called it *live eyes*—when a player is active, engaged, totally locked in. At Bowling Green, it's taken on our mascot: *Falcon Eyes*.

Falcon Eyes stay wide open when the pressure intensifies. They scan the field with panoramic awareness and then bore in like a predator on a single target. They don't flinch or blink. In our locker room, I'll post photos from big defining sports moments: Tiger Woods stalking a Sunday putt, Michael Jordan sizing up the last shot, Tom Brady over the ball with the entire stadium leaning forward, Ray Lewis before a fourth and one. If you look at their faces, no matter what's on the scoreboard, their eyes don't move. Their eyes tell the huddle, "Give it to me."

There's a reason the falcon metaphor works. A falcon has a protective inner eyelid—a built-in shield—so it can slice through the air at impossible speed and still see clearly. The great ones in sport have their own version of that third eyelid: a calm that drops over the moment. Noise hits them, but their focus filters it. The game accelerates, so their vision sharpens.

Every year, I ask our guys, "Who has Falcon Eyes?" They throw out names like LeBron, Kobe, Serena, Nadal, you name it. The list changes, but the trait doesn't. Competitive eyes do three things:

- **Invite the moment.** They don't shrink in the fourth quarter. They grow. Those eyes are saying, "Ball here."
- **Hold focus under fire.** They track chaos and still find the one read that matters.
- **Transmit belief.** One look in the huddle says, "We're fine. Follow me."

That's what we train. We lift and we sprint and we script plays, but every rep is also teaching the eyes—resetting them after a mistake, hardening them through preparation, widening them to see the whole picture, and then narrowing them to finish. You earn Falcon Eyes in the hard reps when nobody's clapping.

CLUTCH IS FOCUS

People love to talk about talent when the game's on the line. I don't. I talk about focus.

We were in the Alamo Bowl at Wisconsin, down late to Colorado. It was the fourth quarter, the last drive. We had to cover eighty yards or the season would end. Our quarterback was Brooks Bollinger—one of the finest competitors I've ever coached. If I had to be someone other than myself, I'd pick Brooks. He was a great leader, a great teammate—all of it.

Brooks Bollinger leading the Badgers to an
improbable fourth-quarter comeback victory
against Colorado in the Alamo Bowl
(Photo © Wisconsin Athletics—David Stluka)

His drive was not a showcase of arm talent or a magic playbook. It was a masterclass in focus. We hit a fourth and nineteen. Then a fourth and ten. No flinch. No blink. His eyes remained steady, his operation clean. The huddle felt it—*we're fine*. And on the last play of regulation, quarterback draw, Brooks knifed through the line, carried the ball across the goal line, and tied the game. We won in overtime.

What made it clutch was his attention to the moment. He had a presence under pressure. His feet were right, his eyes right, so his decisions were right. When the noise in the stadium got louder, his world and his focus got smaller. That's what focus does. It filters chaos and amplifies execution.

As I teach our guys, when everything speeds up, *you* slow down. Build that skill every day through film habits, cadence discipline, protection

checks, and situational awareness. Like I said, you don't rise to the occasion; you fall to your training. Brooks did. That's why he could autograph the moment.

EYES THAT DON'T BLINK

Some players don't just play the game—they bend it to their will through focus. Let me give you three examples, all different positions, all prolific players from Wisconsin—Ron Dayne, Joe Thomas, and Lee Evans.

Ron Dayne, even as a freshman, was a force of nature in a college kid's body. Over four of the final five regular-season games, he ran with reckless abandon and dominated down the stretch. He gashed Purdue for thirty carries and 244 yards; battered Minnesota with fifty carries for 297 yards; followed with a memorable forty-one-carry, 289-yard performance against Illinois; and closed the regular season with thirty-six carries for 339 yards at Hawaii. That was focus and sheer will. I like to call it "live eyes," competitive eyes, winning eyes. Eyes that don't blink.

When everyone else's legs got heavy and plodding, his focus got sharper. He didn't blink through snap after snap, yard after yard, until

Ron Dayne running for the record books
(Photo © Wisconsin Athletics—David Stluka)

he willed our team into a bowl game. The stat lines were ridiculous, of course, but what made him special wasn't just the production; it was the tenacity in his stare between plays. It was a stare that said, "Give me the ball again." That's what competitive eyes look like.

Then there's *Lee Evans*. It was 2003, Ohio State, a night game in a torrential downpour. Our starting quarterback took a shot to the throat and couldn't speak, so we went with the backup, Lee. We didn't throw much because it's hard to throw when the sky's dumping water and the ball feels like a cinder block.

At halftime, I told Lee, "Hang in there. We'll get you the ball."

He just nodded and said, "Coach, I'll be ready when you call my number."

Across from him all night was Chris Gamble—an all-American, first-round talent. Through three and a half quarters, Lee didn't have a catch.

With the ball on our twenty, we dialed an out-and-up—what we called a *jerk route*. Gamble jumped the out; Lee drifted right by him and sprinted eighty yards into the end zone. The stadium erupted. Lee

*Lee Evans and his trademark eyes not blinking and finishing a catch against
all-American Carlos Rogers in the 2003 Music City Bowl
(Photo © Wisconsin Athletics—David Stluka)*

stayed present all night. He showed patience without passivity and focus
without frustration, so when his number got called, he was able to finish.

Lee was the true pro. He was relaxed under pressure, his eyes always
wide, framing the moment while the rest of us endured the storm.

Joe Thomas was the trifecta—prodigious talent, all-American, and
first-round draft pick. At six six, with coast-to-coast arms, ballerina feet,
and a relentlessly curious mind, he was the prototypical franchise left
tackle, the guardian of the quarterback's blind side. He made it look
effortless because no one prepared harder: copious notes on every rusher's tells, tendencies, and counters, then a personal plan to neutralize
their fastball, curve, and changeup. He played with "winning eyes"—
eyes that don't blink—where elite talent met elite preparation. In the
NFL, he became the iron man, logging 10,363 consecutive snaps. A
unanimous All-American at Wisconsin, the 2007 No. 3 overall pick, a
10-time Pro Bowler, six-time First-Team All-Pro, and a 2023 first-ballot

Joe Thomas—all-American and first-ballot
NFL Hall of Famer (Photo © Wisconsin
Athletics—David Stluka)

Hall of Famer—Joe Thomas was built for greatness and backed it up with relentless focus.

Joe Thomas with those steady eyes, winning eyes, "Eyes that don't blink"

That's the lesson I want our guys to take: *Clutch isn't talent; clutch is attention.* Dayne taught us that endurance is a choice you make every snap. Evans taught us that silence can set up the loudest play of the night. Joe Thomas taught us that steady eyes that can concentrate for extraordinary amounts of time are winning eyes. They are "eyes that refuse to blink." So keep your eyes open when the game tries to make you blink. Be patient and present, and when the door finally opens, run through it and seize the moment.

TEACH THE EYES TO STAY OPEN

We train concentration and presence under pressure because there will always be a single moment—maybe one snap all night—when a player's number gets called and the entire game hinges on their response. You don't pick the timing. You only pick your readiness.

Pressure is loud. It throws static in your head, but the great ones don't let the noise in. They remain clear and engaged. That's why Lee Evans could go three and a half quarters in a downpour without a target and still explode when the ball finally came his way. If he had listened to the noise, the headline the next day would've been about an all-American getting erased. Instead, he stayed present, and when the door opened, he ran through it.

Presence under pressure is an obligation. People in the stands paid to watch you perform. Teammates in the huddle depend on you to do your job with poise and polish. It's stewardship of your role.

Our job as coaches is to build that presence on purpose, so we script stress into practice through sudden-change periods, crowd noise, fourth-and-must scenarios, two-minute drills, backed-up coming out, and red zone with no timeouts. We rehearse communication, cadence, protection checks, ball security, and the next-play reset until they're automatic. We praise habits, and we make pressure familiar, so game day feels like a replay.

Here's the standard:

- Eliminate distractions. Control your eyes and breathing, focus on the assignment. What's the call? What's the key? What's the finish?
- Play the next play. If you make a mistake, reset immediately. Poise is recovery speed.
- Welcome the moment. When it gets late and loud, let your focus expand to the picture and narrow to the task. *Ball here.*

Teach the eyes to stay open. Train concentration until it's a reflex. Then, when the moment arrives, you won't need a speech. You'll have your preparation and your poise, ready to seize the play.

FALCON EYES OFF THE FIELD

Falcon Eyes don't retire when the clock hits zero. They travel with you into boardrooms, kitchens, classrooms, and late-night, lights-off conversations. The trait is the same everywhere: *sustained concentration under pressure*. See what matters. Block what doesn't. Finish the task in front of you with poise.

In business, the best executives lock onto the next right action and execute it—email by email, meeting by meeting—while everyone else is running around. Call it *task gravity*. Focus on the task at hand, define it, do it, repeat. Results follow people who can keep their eyes open when distractions try to steal their attention.

In relationships, Falcon Eyes look past the surface and find the deeper reality. You listen all the way through, not just until it's your turn to talk. You read the room, the mood, the moment. You notice the small tells, such as fatigue in a voice or hesitation in a sentence, and you respond with presence, not performance. It's love in action that says, "I'm here. I'm locked in. You matter."

In parenting, Falcon Eyes are nonnegotiable, especially when your kids are young. You track the whole field: homework, heart, habits, friends. You don't parent on autopilot. You parent with attention. You don't let your gaze drift to the phone when your child is sharing with you about their day. You scan wide to keep them safe, then lock tight to teach, correct, or celebrate. If you want influence in their teenage years, earn it now with focused presence.

Here's how to build Falcon Eyes anywhere:

- Name the task. What exactly must be done in the next ten minutes? Clarity narrows chaos.
- Control your inputs. Cut the noise—alerts, tabs, excuses. Attention is a competitive advantage.
- Breathe and reset. One mistake isn't a spiral. Focus on the next play.
- Finish clean. Poise + polish = trust. Trust compounds into opportunity.

Champions in any arena carry the same look: their eyes focused, vision wide when it needs to be, needle-point sharp when it must be. Bring those eyes to your career. Bring them to your marriage. Bring them to your kids. When the moments that matter arrive—and they will—you won't need perfect conditions. You'll need open eyes and the courage to seize the moment.

CHAPTER EIGHT

DREAM. PLAN. ACTIVATE. ACHIEVE.

DREAMS ARE THE ignition. They light the fire. They give you a picture of a future that doesn't exist yet and dare you to go build it. That's why I tell my players, my staff, and my kids, "Never apologize for a big dream."

I prefer championship dreams, confetti-falling dreams, the kind that make you wake up with your heart already sprinting. Big dreamers don't just imagine the world, they move it.

But dreams without a plan evaporate the minute the alarm clock goes off. If inspiration is a spark, a blueprint turns that spark into a bonfire. In football, we would never run onto the field with only a hope and a hunch. We carry a call sheet, a scouting report, a scripted open, and contingency answers for every look we might get. That's respect for the dream.

Activation is the separator. You can have the right vision and the right plan, but if you don't activate it daily, deliberately, relentlessly, then nothing happens. Activation is when you take the blueprint off the whiteboard and grind it into reality. It's when you show up on a Tuesday in November, when no one's watching, and execute the next rep on the plan. One meeting, one drill, one page, one phone call—string enough of those together and people call it momentum. I call it doing your job.

If you want a picture of what this feels like, talk to a construction crew. They show up with a set of plans and march through them. They pour the footings, frame the walls, set the windows, raise the roof. They get to see and experience tangible progress, step by step. That creates pride and satisfaction because every day has a target, and every target gets hit. That's what a good life feels like when you're working a good plan.

If you want a warning, look at the history of professional football leagues that tried to compete with the NFL (e.g., XFL, World Football League). Did they have big dreams? Absolutely, but many were littered with beautiful slogans and thin blueprints. Vision alone won't beat structure. If your plan can't survive budget, talent, operations, and execution, you don't have a league.

So here's my coaching point for every arena of life, whether careers, relationships, parenting, or faith:

1. *Dream* with audacity. See it in color. Name the scoreboard.
2. *Plan* with precision. Put dates, roles, and checkpoints on paper.
3. *Activate* with discipline. Daily actions, no skipped steps, no excuses.
4. *Achieve* with humility. Then reset the goal and go again.

Most people stall between Plan and Activate. They want the feeling of progress without the cost of progress. Not my team. In our locker room, activation is nonnegotiable. It's how you transform "someday" into "we did it."

Write the blueprint, then work the blueprint. Adjust the blueprint as needed, but don't you dare leave it on the clipboard. Activate it today.

Then activate it again tomorrow. Then the day after that. That's how dreams stop being dreams and start becoming history.

THE BRIDGE TO ACHIEVEMENT

Activation is what puts your plan in play. It's where vision leaves the whiteboard and steps onto the field. Dreams are aspirations, but activation is perspiration. It's sweat equity, invested over and over until compound interest shows up as progress you can feel. You don't need perfect conditions. You just need a do-whatever-it-takes attitude and a willingness to work.

Teddy Roosevelt said the best prize life offers is "the chance to work hard at work worth doing." That's activation in one sentence.

On the road to "activation," expect traffic, detours, and construction zones. Expect days that are lonely, dark, and confusing. That's the road less traveled because it demands belief strong enough to stretch you further than you've ever been stretched. Do more. Then do more again. Keep stretching. Keep reaching. Reps build results. Results build belief. Belief fuels the next rep.

You will get knocked down. That's OK. Get up and keep swinging, from sunup to sundown if that's what it takes. If you believe in your dream, keep swinging. Wake up flying. Open your call sheet. Execute the next play. Follow your personal roadmap with stubborn consistency. Stack enough green-light days—days where you choose to press on and attack—and momentum becomes your teammate.

Activation is a habit that looks like this:

- You set the target and time stamp it.
- You run your script even when the feelings fade.
- You correct mid-drive without losing the chains.
- You own the day before the day owns you.

Your attitude matters. A positive attitude gives you a competitive advantage because it keeps your eyes up, your feet moving, and your hands ready for the next assignment. In our locker room, every day is a green-light day with permission granted to advance the ball. We play the down in front of us no matter what.

Dream. Plan. Activate. Achieve. That's the sequence. Most people stop at planning and call it progress. Not us. We activate relentlessly, repeatedly, and with joy because we know what's on the other side of that bridge: the confetti, the handshake line, celebration in the locker room, and the satisfaction of work worth doing.

Take the first step today. Then take the next. Keep taking them until the scoreboard tells the story you already believed.

CONSTRUCTION WORKERS VERSUS DESTRUCTION WORKERS

Construction Workers
- Have a vision, a plan, and a blueprint they follow with pride and precision.
- Diligently follow the plan—see the big picture and how they fit into it (know their role).
- Master the fundamentals: every nail, every corner— measure, level, and do it right.
- Build—always building people up; positive, supportive, unselfish, and selfless.
- Feel fulfilled—experience the highest job satisfaction.
- Take responsibility for their job and do it to the best of their ability—with passion and pride.
- Build from the ground up—start with a strong foundation.

- Handle adversity—adjust to the weather, confront issues, and solve problems.
- Focus on daily achievement—make progress and improve every day.
- "Wake up flying" and attack the day with purpose and clear objectives.
- Work together—share the load and express gratitude.
- Bring energy—upbeat, optimistic people.
- Stay lively, interested, engaged, and focused—Falcon Eyes and great body language.
- Know how to finish—own the fourth quarter.
- Celebrate together—because it's always a team effort.

Destruction Workers
- Have no plan—no vision.
- Live day to day—meal to meal.
- Take shortcuts—the easy way.
- Implode—tear people down; selfish, negative, and quick to revel in others' failures.
- Never fulfilled—always make excuses; it's always someone else's fault.
- Avoid responsibility at all costs—"let someone else do it."
- Destroy from the top down—show total disregard for others.
- Crumble when times are tough—run from problems; can't solve anything on their own.
- Procrastinate—"wait till tomorrow" mentality.
- Keep hitting the snooze button.
- Hoard everything—ungrateful.
- Always tired and yawning.
- Dull, wandering, listless eyes.

- Glass is always half empty.
- Sleep in.
- Can't get anything accomplished.
- Find ways to delay the project finish date.
- Celebrate alone.

DREAMERS WHO CHANGED THEIR WORLD

When I talk about dreamers, I'm not talking about wishful thinking. I'm talking about people who see a future that doesn't exist yet and then activate a plan so fiercely that the rest of us end up living in their vision.

Think about Steve Jobs. He didn't stand around asking focus groups for permission. He believed people often don't know what they need until you show it to them. That's not arrogance. That's imagination with a work ethic. He failed, got knocked down, rebuilt, rallied a team around a bold picture, and changed how we communicate, learn, work, and play. That's what happens when a dream is paired with relentless activation. Tinkering becomes technology. Curiosity becomes culture. A sketch on a napkin becomes a device the whole world carries in its pocket. Vision, plan, activate—repeat.

And then there's Bill Russell, the greatest champion the NBA has ever seen. He earned eleven rings as a player. Russell talked about something I love: the imagination quotient. Everybody measures IQ, EQ, and AQ, but he pressed us to measure curiosity—the willingness to envision a different outcome and then stretch yourself until it's real. That was Russell's advantage. He saw the court differently. He defended differently. He led differently. He imagined a way to win, and then he did the hard, unglamorous work to make that imagination the team's reality. That's activation wearing high-tops.

Great dreamers are great activators. They don't just dream in color. They schedule the dream. They write the blueprint. They stack green-light days one rep at a time.

That's our play, too. Dream with audacity. Plan with precision. Activate with discipline. Achieve with humility. Wake up flying, execute your game plan, follow your personal roadmap, and keep stretching. Curiosity is your engine, and work is your bridge, so cross it.

GRIT TO GRIND

You don't grind just to grind—you grind because you believe in what you're trying to achieve. Belief gives the work its weight. It connects you to something you will not compromise when the day gets tough and the scoreboard isn't on your side.

Start with core values you can say out loud and live out loud. In our locker room it's *grit, gratitude, loyalty,* and *selflessness.* Those are some big words, but they only matter if you practice them daily, teach them, model them, and guard them. When you're rooted in values you trust, the hard parts stop feeling like punishment and start feeling like purpose.

Habits are how belief becomes muscle:

- *Focus and concentration.* Football games last three and a half hours. Championships demand months of that same attention. Bring Falcon Eyes with long-haul focus, one snap at a time.
- *Do it right, then do it right again.* Excellence is repetition. Tiger Woods calls it "repeating the swing." We call it running the right play over and over until it isn't luck but identity.
- *Know the one fundamental that moves you through the stall.* When pressure intensifies, return to your base: stance, breath, first step, eyes. Simplicity under stress wins.

- *Wring the towel.* Wring every ounce of sweat out of the cloth. Sweat equity is the best equity because it's earned, never given. Leave no work unwrung.
- *Persistence and perseverance.* You will get knocked down. Get back up. You will get outflanked. Adjust. Keep swinging from sunup to sundown if that's what the mission requires.

Belief fuels grit; grit shapes habits; habits carry you through the grind. Wake up flying. Open your plan. Execute the next rep with your values in the huddle. Stack green-light days—focus, repeat the swing, wring the towel—and watch the stall give way to momentum.

That's how we build the grit to grind, with convictions you won't trade, habits you won't skip, and a willingness to keep swinging until the dream becomes reality.

WHAT GRIT IS

- Grit is never giving up and never giving in.
- Grit is getting knocked down and always getting back up.
- Grit is "wringing the towel" for every ounce of sweat we drop—because "sweat equity is the best equity": earned, never given.
- Grit is *#WakingUpFlying*—attacking the day and meeting all challenges head-on.
- Grit is living the mantra *#GreenMeansGo*—full throttle, pedal to the metal—*#FalconUp* to *#FalconDown*. Every day is a *#GreenlightDay*. Falcon fast!
- Grit is belief—believing in yourself when everyone doubts you.

- Grit is the ability to persevere when times are tough; playing the next play with incredible focus and passion when the previous play was negative.
- Grit is resolve and absolute conviction in who you are, how you live, and what you want to achieve.
- Grit is tenacity—the scratching and clawing that life demands. Always scratching. Always clawing. Because that's life.
- Grit is navigating the unexpected traffic jams, detours, construction zones, and roadblocks—and still finding a way to reach your destination.
- Grit is work—demanding work that requires relentless commitment to doing your job and doing it with pride, passion, and purpose.
- Grit is getting your hands dirty, your face dirty, your whole body dirty—and loving it.
- Grit is the orange and brown blood that flows through all Falcons—this is who we are.
- Grit always wins.

CHAPTER NINE

BREAKING DOWN THE WALLS

YOU CHANGE A culture by changing the conversations. Every "-ism" that divides—racism, sexism, ageism, classism—shrinks when real people talk, listen, and stay in the huddle long enough to understand one another. Dialogue is the demolition crew. Communication is the sledgehammer. Proximity is the door we walk through together.

Dr. King taught a simple chain reaction: we fear what we don't know; we don't know what we don't talk to; and when we finally talk, fear loses its grip. That's the locker room at its best. A football locker room is a crash course in humanity, with all ages, races, backgrounds, and faiths jammed into one space with a common mission and a shared clock. You learn fast that blood runs the same color and respect sounds the same in any accent. When you sweat together, fail together, rise together, win together, celebrate together, the walls come down.

I call it turning "-isms" into "-hoods." *Racism* becomes *brotherhood* when men work, sacrifice, and win together. *Sexism* becomes *sisterhood* when women are given full voice, full respect, and full value in the room. *Ageism* becomes *neighborhood* when generations link arms, putting wisdom beside energy, experience beside hunger. Even *elitism* yields to *teammate-hood* when no one stands above the team and everyone pulls the rope together.

So, open the huddle and make room for voices you haven't heard. Listen past the headline and ask the follow-up question that invites a story instead of a slogan. Share the load on something that costs both sides in service, tough practices, or real goals, because shared strain builds trust faster than speeches ever will. Name the standard (e.g., respect, dignity, truth) and hold it without exceptions or favorites. Break bread together because tables turn teammates into family. And when it's awkward, stay in it anyway. Growth lives on the far side of discomfort, and so does unity.

Jaison Patterson's uncle Jerry said it best: "Real is real, real is rare, and real has no color." I love that line because it cuts through every label. Real shows up. Real makes room in the pew and at the dinner table. Real says, "You're with us," and then proves it with time, effort, and consistency.

We won't fix the world by shouting labels across a field. We'll fix it by living loyalties inside the locker room, the company, and the family one conversation at a time, rep by rep, week after week. Do that, and the walls eventually crumble. That's the mission of any great team. Turn the "-isms" that divide us into the "-hoods" that unite us. Real is real. Real is rare. And when it's real, it wins.

THE ANTIDOTES TO DIVISION

Fear thrives where conversation dies. We're living in a moment where folks would rather shout labels than speak names. My first instruction is always, "Throw your politics out the window before you walk into the huddle. These are human beings. Start there."

This summer in Seattle, I cut through a park and watched a pack of five-to-eight-year-olds racing around and having fun together. They were every shade of skin, every background, every family story, and they were all laughing, chasing, conquering the monkey bars like it was a recess world championship. Nobody paused to run a background check on beliefs. Nobody split into camps. Without anyone telling them to, they became teammates. That's the natural state of the human heart before we teach it to be suspicious.

I don't believe we are born to hate. I think we are taught to hate. Indoctrination fills the silence when we stop talking, and that's the tragedy. Most people—call it 85 percent—are decent and want to help. They want to belong and come together. It's the loud 15 percent, the monsters made by echo chambers and isolation, who profit from the division. The antidote isn't more noise or more division. It's communication with a name and a face.

This is why I believe in the locker room. In the locker room, you put people shoulder to shoulder with a shared mission and a shared clock, and the labels start losing steam. Conversation replaces caricature. Effort replaces accusation. Respect replaces suspicion. Fear can't survive when you look each other in the eye, learn each other's stories, sweat through the same drills, and break bread afterward.

So choose people over posture. Sit down. Ask a second question. Stay long enough to hear an answer that doesn't fit your script. In our program, we refuse to let silence do the teaching. We communicate until fear has nowhere left to hide. That's how teams win, families heal, and communities remember what those kids at the park already know: we were made to play together.

Brotherhood, sisterhood, motherhood, fatherhood, and servanthood each carry the same heartbeat: love. Love is the antidote to hatred, to ignorance, to the fractures that split teams, companies, and families. In our world, it starts on the floor of the locker room. That concrete is poured with love, earned through sweat, trust, accountability, and the belief that every person in the huddle matters.

Brotherhood is the bond forged by shared struggle. It says, "Your success is my responsibility." Sisterhood brings full voice and full value; it refuses to let anyone sit on the margins. Fatherhood offers guidance and guardrails—strength with tenderness, truth with patience. Motherhood nurtures, fiercely protects and ultimately fills their children with "the human touch." And servanthood threads them all together. It reverses the pecking order. It takes the towel in the fourth quarter and washes feet. When you embrace servanthood, you stop performing for attention and start playing for a higher purpose. That's where unity takes root.

The goal is far bigger than a good season or a championship ring. The real win is when what we build in here becomes a way of life out there—when brotherhood and sisterhood spill into neighborhoods, when streets and schools and workplaces become places of safety instead of suspicion. I want teams that graduate into communities where people of every race and religion can live without fear, where a shared table replaces separate corners, where love becomes the operating system instead of the exception.

It all starts with appreciation and understanding. Start seeing the person, not the label. Choose to listen long enough for respect to grow. Choose service over status. That's the mission: build a brotherhood, honor a sisterhood, practice fatherhood, exalt motherhood, and live servanthood. Love takes the field, and when love takes the field, it changes the score.

HOW FOOTBALL PULLS US TOGETHER

If you want to see the division lose its grip, stand on a high school sideline on a Friday night. The band tunes up, the sun drops behind the bleachers, and a whole town of parents, grandparents, teachers, little brothers, and girlfriends funnels into one place with one heart and soul. Football has a way of turning scattered lives into a single huddle. It asks us to show up together, work together, cheer together, and, when it's over, to carry that together into the week.

I've watched it start with something as simple as a meal. My wife helps organize the pregame dinners on Thursday night and Friday afternoon, where we feed a hundred teenage boys like clockwork. You want a crash course in unity? Try coordinating that circus. Parents who barely knew each other became a team, sharing shopping lists, crockpots, allergy charts, pickup vans, and prayer over the food. In the process, they stopped being "Jake's mom" or "Noah's dad" and started becoming family, shoulder to shoulder around a table, serving the same mission.

Football also brought LaMartinez Walker into our lives. A thirty-year-old African American man from Gainesville, he has become part of our family. We met LaMartinez when Urban Meyer hired me to coach at the University of Florida. He was fourteen then, connected to us through the team's mentoring program. "L," as everyone knows him, bonded immediately with Cassi and Jackson, and a true big-brotherhood formed.

Cassi, Jackson, Muzzi, and "L" in a family picture (Photo © Salli White)

Jackson, Cassi, and "L" in Las Vegas, celebrating our twentieth anniversary (Photo © Brian White)

He later stood as best man in my son's wedding, and he's still "L" to all of us. People hear that and reach for a movie script—"It's like *Blind Side 2*," they say—but they've got it backward. L impacted us as much as we impacted him. That's the beauty of a locker room done right: the human touch, values handed down by parents, teachers, and coaches, meeting a young man's grit and gratitude at exactly the right time.

Years after we left Florida, that bond stayed strong. In fact, my ninety-year-old mother-in-law, "Granny," and L kept going to church together every weekend. There's a photo of them arm-in-arm at Triple Cross Church in Micanopy. It's a cowboy church, which means worship is done outdoors with horses in the background.

Granny even posted that photo, with the caption, "This is my grandson, L. He calls me Granny." That's love with a face and a name. That's what

This is L and me at TRIPLE CROSS
CHURCH. There is not a better person
than L. I am Granny to him , and he's my
grandson.

"L" and Granny sharing time together at
Triple Cross Cowboy Church in Florida
(Photo © Jean Bunch)

happens when you choose proximity over posture and relationship over
rhetoric. It happened because football introduced us, then love did the rest.

This is bigger than one family. In Florida, Texas, California—pick
your zip code—Friday night is a civic holiday. The lights click on, the
pageantry rolls out, and the town remembers how to be a community.
It's the one place where the banker and the bricklayer, the freshman and
the retired math teacher, sit ten feet apart and care about the same thing
at the same time. Don't underestimate what that does for a country.

Football can be brutal and beautiful in the same breath, but at its
best, it heals. It turns strangers into neighbors, teammates into brothers,
and a game into a glue strong enough to hold a community together.

WORK WORTH DOING

Coaching is work worth doing because it changes people in real
time, one practice, one conversation, one hard truth, and one

arm-around-the-shoulder at a time. I've never felt like I've worked a day in my life as a coach. It's perpetual recess with a purpose. I wake up at four, get the workout in, head to the facility, grind twelve to fifteen hours, come home, sleep, and do it all over again—not because I have to, but because I love to.

Thirty years, and my wife has never heard me say, "I dread going in today." How could I? I get to help young men discover who they are and what they can be.

People remember how you make them feel. Players I've coached may not quote my speeches, but they'll remember the energy and the optimism. They'll say, "Coach was positive. The coach was fun to be around. The coach made me feel like I could do hard things." That matters. That changes lives. I'm a glass-half-full guy thanks to my mom, who could find the silver lining in a thunderstorm, and that lens influenced the locker room atmosphere. I want my locker room to be upbeat, demanding, and hopeful.

The legacy of a life spent in the locker room isn't trophies or awards. It's phone calls. Holidays ring with voices that once wore our team colors. It's Christmas texts and Thanksgiving voicemails that say, "Coach, you changed my life." That's the scoreboard I care about.

This week, I received a group text from one of my dad's former players, Tommy Cassidy, who was seven years older than me, over fifty years removed from his playing days. He sent a picture of a sunset with a simple line: "Thinking of Coach." Then the thread lit up with teammates Dave Ramsey and Joe Finnegan reflecting on the big smile, the positive energy, the confidence my father put in their souls. Half a century later, and they're still carrying his belief. That's legacy.

Coaching is a sacred trust. We borrow young hearts for a few seasons and try to send them back stronger, more disciplined, more courageous, more sure of who they are. We teach them to chase excellence, to serve others, to love the brother beside them, to fight for something bigger

8:55

TC

Tom

Thinking of Coach on my walk home.

Good thoughts in solitude.

Think of how he conducted the team...but more the individual interactions he had with each of us...genuine interest... sincere....motivating...always finishing with that big smile. Good for you Tommy

Coach's passion for life was infectious. Absolutely had a positive impact on all our lives. Propelled us forward with more confidence as well as an appreciation to enjoy the ride. We were blessed.

That is awesome....made my day......how cool is it that we r all connected over 50 years later

iMessage

TC

Tom

Brian...whenever I see you I think of the joy that your brothers and sister had being with your dad and around the team. Longfellow "the thoughts of youth are long, long thoughts."

Amen, kid

So cool & thanks so much for the wonderful memories of a treasured childhood than a stat line. If we do it right, they leave with a compass to guide the rest of their lives.

So why is this work worth doing? Because the world needs men who know how to lead with joy, persevere with grit, and lift others while they climb. The legacy is written in the lives of players who become better husbands, fathers, teammates, neighbors. It's the sunset text to a coach long after the lights are off and the crowd is gone. It's the echo of a locker room that taught them to believe, and a life that proves they still do.

Being a coach means waking up every day trying to recapture something no other job can manufacture—that surge of energy, the authenticity and unfiltered reality of a team bound together by one mission. Even now, the hair rises on my arms just talking about it. I've worked other jobs, but nothing comes close to what the locker room creates when it's alive and honest and all in.

The locker room is pure spontaneity and pure truth. It's the blast of joy after a hard-earned win, the roar that starts in the soles of your feet and travels through the rafters. And it's the quiet after a gutting loss, when a teammate finds you in the tunnel, puts a hand on your shoulder, and reminds you that you are not alone. Those lows etch as deep as the highs, and, somehow, they mean just as much because in those moments you learn what brotherhood really costs and what it's worth.

It's joy that refuses to fade, the passion that refuels you, the energy that keeps calling you back to the huddle. The locker room teaches you to celebrate with humility and to grieve with grace. It trains your heart to compete without losing its tenderness. It stamps you with memories that outlast the scoreboard, with faces, voices, laughter, the ring of cleats on concrete, the feel of an arm around your neck when words won't do.

I've spent my life chasing that feeling, chasing the authenticity and the joy the locker room gives so freely to those who give themselves to it. If I'm remembered for anything, let it be this: I loved the locker room. I believed in the men inside it. And I never stopped chasing the magic that only a locker room can make.

WHY THE LOCKER ROOM IS SACRED

THE LOCKER ROOM is sacred because it holds the values of a team in one living space. It's where the truth of an organization shows up without polish—authenticity in its rawest form. You can't recreate it in a conference room or a classroom. The locker room is organic. When it's healthy, it grows like something wild and good— trust takes root, accountability finds its voice, love shows up as work. When it's right, it's a kind of music: a hundred different instruments creating a harmony you feel in your soul.

I've seen the other side, too. There are locker rooms out of tune, where people are spoiled, splintered, and talking past each other. Those rooms don't win because they don't share values or a vision. They don't pull the rope in the same direction. They mistake talent for chemistry and slogans for standards. That division shows up on Friday night, every time.

But when a locker room is harmonic—when love and truth and toughness live at the same address—it's rare and worth fighting for. You chase it, you protect it, you demand it, because what happens in that space is indescribable. After an incredible win, the euphoria that erupts, with players laughing, crying, hugging, shouting, feels like someone opened a door to something bigger than a game. And after a crushing loss, the arm around a shoulder, the look in a teammate's eyes, the unspoken promise to go again, that's sacred, too. It's the sound of a kill choosing each other, even when it hurts.

If you could bottle that feeling, you'd change cities. You'd change lives. That's why the locker room remains sacred. It's the one place where our highest ideals get stress-tested and proven true, where strangers become brothers, and where a shared purpose turns ordinary people into a team. You can't fake it. You can only build it, protect it, and be grateful you got to stand inside it while it sang.

KEEP THE LOCKER ROOM ALIVE

Carry the locker room with you. Not the walls, of course, but the spirit. Keep spontaneity and authenticity at the center of who you are. The locker room is sacred because it breaks down every boundary and tells the truth without makeup. In that space, frauds get exposed, excuses get silenced, and what's real rises to the surface. That's not just a football thing; that's a life thing.

So make your family room a locker room. Make your boardroom a locker room. Build teams where honesty is expected, loyalty is practiced, and communication is open, direct, and human. Tell the truth even when it costs you. Show up with the same energy on the hard days that you bring on the highlight days. Look each other in the eye. Fight *for* one another, not *with* one another. Celebrate big. Grieve well. Then get back to work together.

You won't replicate the exact electricity of a Saturday night in a football facility, and that's OK. Chase it anyway. It's worth the effort because when you capture even a glimpse of it, you feel something that can't be faked. It changes households. It changes companies. It changes communities. It changed me.

Be real. Be forthright. Be loyal. Keep the conversation going when it would be easier to retreat. Protect the standard. Refuse to let cynicism do the teaching. If you do that—if you carry the locker room into your home, your business, your town—you'll give the people you lead what the locker room gave us: a place where truth and love inhabit the same space, where men and women become better for having belonged, and where the best of us gets called forward on purpose.

That's my final encouragement and my challenge: keep the locker room alive. Let it shape how you speak, how you serve, how you stand together. Do that, and you won't just win seasons—you'll win lives.

ACKNOWLEDGMENTS

GRATITUDE IS A core value for me because this game has given me far more than I could ever pay back. When I look back over the years—the buses and planes, the late nights and early mornings—what I see are the faces and names of people who made my life richer and my calling clearer.

I think back to Fordham and immediately smile: Bobby Hagen, Frank D'Alessio, Tim Murray, Chris Cocozza, Ricky Hollowell, Eddie Pearson, and Rodney "Night Train" Knight—young men who trusted a young coach and let me into their lives. Notre Dame shaped me, and Wisconsin carved something permanent into my soul. Notre Dame was an experience one could only dream of, and it came true. What a group of unforgettable players starting with Tony Rice; Ricky Watters; Tony and Reggie Brooks; Mark Green; Anthony Johnson; Andy Heck; Tim Grunhard; Mike Brennan; Pete Graham; Derek Brown; Raghib "Rocket" Ismail; the charismatic Three Amigos—Frank Stams, Mike Stonebreaker, and Wes Pritchett; Doug DiOrio; and Pat Eilers—one of the most competitive, fiercely driven, and selfless people I have ever met.

Wisconsin was an eleven-year wave that has so many wonderful memories of players who were about the right stuff. Brooks Bollinger was a special leader and person—if I could be any person other than myself, I'd pick Brooks—along with Lee Evans, Joe Thomas, John Sigmund, Mark Anelli, Tony Paciotti, Chris Chambers, Chris McIntosh, Aaron Gibson, Ron Dayne, Eddie Faulkner, Brandon Williams, Carl McCullough, Jonathon Clinkscale, Kalvin Barrett, Jason Palermo, Donnel Thompson, Mark Tauscher, Kevin Stemke, Matt Davenport, Jim Sorgi, John Stocco, Casey Rabach, Al Johnson, Cecil Martin, Garrett Graham, Chris Pressley, P.J. Hill, Matt Unertl, Owen Daniels, Jim Leonhard, Donte King, Greg Root, Chad Kuhns, Russ Kuhns, Michael Bennett, Anthony Davis, Brian Calhoun, and the unforgettable Matt Bernstein.

Syracuse brought another wave of competitors and friends: Perry Patterson, J.J. Neshewait, Mike Williams, Tony Fiammetta, Justin Outten, Curtis Brinkley, Max Meisel, and Delone Carter. Washington will always be remembered for Mike Gottlieb—one of the hardest-working players I ever coached—and the amazing talent and humility of Jake Locker. Florida gave me the chance to be around greatness—Tim Tebow—and to coach talents like Aaron Hernandez (a remarkable player with incredible work habits but tragic flaws, reminding me that coaching is about the whole person, not just the stat line), Chris Rainey, Jeff Demps, Mike Gillislee, Matt Jones, Kelvin Taylor, John Brantley, Trey Burton, Clay Burton, Jordan Reed, Mark Herndon, Jeff Driskel, Jacoby Brissett, Steve Wilks, Mike and Maurkice Pouncey, Mack Brown, Rick Burgess, Justin Trattou, Duke Lemmens, Riley Cooper, Alex Anzalone, Ronald Powell, Dominique Easley, and Sharrif Floyd. They all made me better.

UNLV is extra special to me. Head coach Jim Strong gave me my first shot to see if I measured up in the "big time." Jeff Horton mentored me when I was green, showed me the ropes in recruiting, believed in me, and later hired me. What a guy, what a coach, what a friend. I met my wife there—how do you measure that gift?—and I found lifelong friends through recruiting, like Demond Thompkins, Omar Love, Jason Davis, Nick Garritano, Brian Parvin, Jon Denton, Jason Toohey, and Todd Floyd—men I still hear from and am proud to know. Paul Pucciarelli, our equipment manager, became my best friend.

Boston College meant working with dear friends—Steve Addazio and Frank Leonard—stacking more memories and more lessons. Coaching and recruiting great players like A.J. Dillon and Zay Flowers—respectively the all-time leading rusher and receiver in school history—was a blast. Connecting with the amazing Ciaffoni family through the recruitment of Mike Ciaffoni—father Joe has become a dear friend, mom Sue, sisters Emma and Bella, and brother Nick have become family. Colorado State is a reel of memory shots: the Rockies, beating Wyoming in the Border War for the Bronze Boot, and being around greatness again in tight end Trey McBride. Trey won the John Mackey Award as the nation's best tight end and is now an All-Pro for the Arizona Cardinals.

Bowling Green, these last four years, has been a joy, full stop. The Toledo rivalry—the Battle of I-75—is special, and beating them three times is unforgettable. The win over Georgia Tech, locker rooms that shook with celebration, and teams that refused to crumble when things got tough are all etched in my mind as "memory shots." Most important has been the lived loyalty of my dear friend Scot Loeffler and his wife, Amie, who accommodated my needs so I could successfully battle Parkinson's disease and still coach at an elite level.

And then there's home. For three decades, my wife has been the center of our program life—Thursday cookies, pregame meals, barbecues, those "Cooking with Coach" moments that turn teams into families. She has fed a hundred boys more times than we can count, and in doing so she taught them what love looks like in casserole form. I'm proud that my players, at every stop, know my wife as "Savage Salli White"—her moniker at Bowling Green. She smooths out my rough edges and spreads the Human Touch to everyone who walks through our door… she knows how to *feed 'em*!

To my children, Cassi and Jackson—thank you from the bottom of my heart for letting me be your dad and for always supporting me, even through the uncomfortable moves. I admire you more than you can imagine, I'm so proud of who you are, and I'm grateful that, from the day you were born, you've shown me that "the human touch always wins."

To my parents, Don and Maureen White—thank you for revealing my life's calling simply by how you lived. Mom, a human hurricane, you showed me what real passion looks like day after day. Dad, you taught me what the "human touch" is and why it always wins.

To my Uncle Bill Linnehan–thank you for always being such an enthusiastic supporter and teaching your nieces and nephews the concept of "Family First"!

To my uncle Gerry White, you taught me what the mantra "Count on Me" really means by living and modeling it for our whole family to witness in real time. I will never forget your steady voice when you came to visit me at Boston College the day after I was diagnosed with Parkinson's disease in June of 2016. I was just about to start coaching a drill and heard your signature "Yo, just want to see how you are doing." You are as real as real can be, and we all know real is rare, and you are *rare*!

To my siblings—thank you for your love and constant validation. Geralyn, the epitome of a doer and the most giving, selfless person I know—a true people mover. Kevin, an iron man filled with grace and competitive greatness—I want you on the line to sink the winning free throws because you always come through in the clutch. Chris, my kindred spirit who let me coach you as you grew up—I can never repay the love you've showered on me.

People ask about trophies, national titles, Rose Bowls. I'm grateful for every single one, but the moments I carry closest aren't made of metal. They're the calls on Christmas and the texts on Thanksgiving. They're the sunset photo from a former player who writes, "Thinking of Coach," and a thread that fills up with memories of a big smile, positive energy, and confidence planted deep. They're the hugs after a win and the arm around a shoulder after a loss. Wins fade, but those kinds of relationships don't.

I've learned lessons that transcend victory and defeat, like gratitude over grievance, optimism over cynicism, service over status, team over self. This game is unforgiving sometimes, but it has given me everything I ever dreamed of and more. I've got countless "memory shots" I'll replay for the rest of my life.

To the players—at Fordham, Notre Dame, Wisconsin, Syracuse, Washington, Florida, UNLV, Boston College, Colorado State, Bowling Green—thank you. You made me better. You trusted me with your hopes and your hard days. You let me teach and, more often than not, you taught me. If I have a legacy, it's that I loved the locker room, I loved the men inside it, and I am profoundly grateful for the joy we built together—joy that outlasts the final whistle and the final record.

ABOUT THE AUTHOR

COACH BRIAN WHITE is a championship-minded leader and master culture-builder with nearly four decades on Division I sidelines. From Fordham to Notre Dame, UNLV, Wisconsin, Syracuse, Washington, Florida, Boston College, Colorado State, and Bowling Green, he's served as position coach, coordinator, and program architect—recruiting, developing, and graduating hundreds of student-athletes while preparing teams for rivalry Saturdays and bowl season. His reputation was earned the hard way, building room-by-room standards, elevating player performance, and aligning staff around a clear, shared identity.

In *The Locker Room Is Not for Sale*, White distills his hard-earned wisdom into a practical playbook for leaders who want results without selling their soul. He writes the way he coaches, with clear standards, high energy, and relentless clarity. Core ideas like "Falcon Eyes" (elite focus), spontaneous authenticity, and everyday grit show leaders how to do tough things well and do them together.

Off the field, Brian advises businesses, schools, and teams on culture, performance, and developing A players. He's a sought-after speaker known for turning big ideas into next-week habits and for reminding audiences that great programs are built on standards.

Coach White lives what he teaches: have fun, keep score, *win*, and leave every locker room, workplace, and family stronger than you found it.

www.ingramcontent.com/pod-product-compliance
Lightning Source LLC
Chambersburg PA
CBHW070717130626
46553CB00005B/2032